THEORIES OF
PROFESSIONAL
LEARNING

A critical guide for teacher educators

Critical Guides for
Teacher Educators

You might also like the following books from Critical Publishing.

Beginning Teacher's Learning: Making Experience Count
By Katharine Burn, Hazel Hagger and Trevor Mutton
978-1-910391-17-4
Published 2015

Developing Creative and Critical Educational Practitioners
By Victoria Door
978-1-909682-37-5
Published 2014

Developing Outstanding Practice in School-based Teacher Education
Edited by Kim Jones and Elizabeth White
978-1-909682-41-2
Published 2014

Dial M for Mentor: Critical Reflections on Mentoring for Coaches, Educators and Trainers
By Jonathan Gravells and Susan Wallace
978-1-909330-00-9
Published 2012

How Do Expert Primary Classteachers Really Work? A Critical guide for Teachers, Headteachers and Teacher Educators
By Tony Eaude
978-1-909330-01-6
Published 2012

Non-directive Coaching: Attitudes, Approaches and Applications
By Bob Thomson
978-1-909330-57-3
Published 2013

Most of our titles are also available in a range of electronic formats. To order please go to our website www.criticalpublishing.com or contact our distributor, NBN International, 10 Thornbury Road, Plymouth PL6 7PP, telephone 01752 202301 or email orders@nbninternational.com.

THEORIES OF
PROFESSIONAL
LEARNING

A critical guide for teacher educators

Series Editor: Ian Menter

Critical Guides for
Teacher Educators

Carey Philpott

First published in 2014 by Critical Publishing Ltd

Reprinted in 2015

British Library Cataloguing in Publication Data
A CIP record for this book is available from the British Library

ISBN: 978-1-909682-33-7

This book is also available in the following e-book formats:
MOBI: 978-1-909682-34-4
EPUB: 978-1-909682-35-1
Adobe e-book reader: 978-1-909682-36-8

Cover and text design by Greensplash Limited
Project Management by Out of House Publishing
Typeset by Newgen Knowledge Works
Printed and bound in Great Britain by 4edge Limited

Critical Publishing
152 Chester Road
Northwich
CW8 4AL

www.criticalpublishing.com

CONTENTS

ACKNOWLEDGEMENTS

For Jan, Katherine and Elizabeth who forfeited their summer holiday so that I could finish this. Also for Patrick, who didn't but who would feel left out if I didn't mention him.

FOREWORD

It has become something of a cliché to say that those of us involved in teacher education 'live in interesting times'. However, such has been the rate of change in many aspects of teacher education in many parts of the world over recent years that this does actually need to be recognised. Because of the global interest in the quality of teaching and the recognition that teacher learning and development plays a crucial part in this, politicians and policymakers have shown increasing interest in the nature of teacher preparation. Early in 2013 the British Educational Research Association (BERA) in collaboration with the Royal Society for the Arts (RSA) established an inquiry into the relationship between research and teacher education. The final report from this inquiry was published in 2014 (BERA/RSA 2014) and sets out a range of findings that include a call for all of those involved – policymakers, practitioners, researchers – *'to exercise leadership amongst their members and partners in promoting the use of evidence, enquiry and evaluation to prioritise the role of research and to make time and resources available for research engagement'* (p 27). One key purpose of this series of *Critical Guides for Teacher Educators* is to provide a resource that will facilitate a concerted move in this direction. The series aims to offer insights for all those with responsibilities in our field to support their critical engagement with practice and policy, through the use of evidence based on research and on experience.

In this particular volume, Carey Philpott provides a very clear introduction to some of the key theories that are currently being used to help us to make sense of the processes of teacher education, initial teacher education in particular. This is an enormously helpful undertaking which he carries out critically and with a view to clear communication of key ideas. In my view, this book will provide many new entrants to the teaching profession – and those involved in supporting them – a clear indication not only of the challenges involved in becoming a teacher, but also of the challenges involved in developing a language through which to understand these complex processes. To take an example of how he provokes critical reflection, I found myself, as someone who has been highly critical of reductionist views of 'teaching as a craft' which is best learned through an apprenticeship model, particularly intrigued to read Carey's cogent articulation of the benefits of a serious and sophisticated adoption of such an approach.

There is always a risk that theory is adopted in a simplistic way that just adds a level of obscurity to discourse. Well, through the very clear linkage he makes with policies and practices in initial teacher education (ITE) and through his reference to a wide range of research, Carey demonstrates how a theoretical approach can offer a crucial enhancement of our rapidly changing professional world.

Ian Menter, Series Editor

Professor of Teacher Education, University of Oxford

October 2014

About the series editor

Ian Menter is Professor of Teacher Education and Director of Professional Programmes in the Department of Education at the University of Oxford. He previously worked at the Universities of Glasgow, the West of Scotland, London Metropolitan, the West of England and Gloucestershire. Before that he was a primary school teacher in Bristol. His most recent publications include *A Literature Review on Teacher Education for the 21st Century* (Scottish Government) and *A Guide to Practitioner Research in Education* (Sage). His work has also been published in many academic journals.

About the author

Carey Philpott was a teacher of English and drama in schools in Glasgow and London. During this time he became involved in teacher education, as a mentor. He later moved to work in teacher education at Oxford Brookes University and the University of Cumbria and is now at the University of Strathclyde. He has been programme leader for a secondary PGCE course, a post-compulsory PGCE course and an undergraduate ITE course. His research interests include professional learning, language and learning, and narrative research.

CRITICAL **ISSUES**

- *What do we want a theory of professional learning to do for us?*
- *What are some of the key differences between professional learning theories?*

Introduction

Theories of professional learning are like lenses that we hope will help us be more effective in supporting the professional learning of our students. We hope that a professional learning theory will give us a more detailed or insightful view of how learning takes place. Part of this more insightful view is identifying what it is that needs to be learned when developing professional abilities. This is because what we need to learn will determine the most effective ways of learning.

In this book, my intention is to set out a critical overview of some different theories of professional learning that have had some influence on Initial Teacher Education (ITE) in recent years. This critical overview is intended as an introduction to the key points of the theories and to some of the main shortcomings, objections to, and developments of each. Each chapter includes suggestions for further reading so that the ideas and arguments can be explored in more detail.

Description or a prescription?

It is worth noting at this stage that providing an insightful account of how professional learning takes place does not lead automatically to providing a prescription for designing professional learning experiences and contexts. Perhaps the most obvious example of this is communities of practice (Chapter 5). In early formulations of communities of practice it seems clear that we are being offered a theory of how professional learning takes place but not a recipe for creating professional learning opportunities or environments. This is because communities of practice were seen as a naturally developing phenomenon rather than one that could be deliberately manufactured.

This can be seen as the first key difference in professional learning theories: are they descriptions, prescriptions, or descriptions that give rise to prescriptions? We might assume that prescriptions are more useful than descriptions, given what we want a theory for, but both have their limitations. Prescriptions, by their very nature, need to simplify what they represent. If they do not they might not be useful. However, this simplification can under-represent what might be important aspects or variables in real life situations. Descriptions may be better able to represent these, and we can reflect ourselves on how we use these descriptions to inform what we do.

Learning theories: a (very) brief history

For learning theories in general, rather than professional learning theories in particular, several related broad historical trajectories can be seen:

> » from a focus on learners as individuals to learning as an irreducibly social process;

> » a broadening of focus from considering conscious knowledge and reasoning to including other aspects of learning such as tacit knowledge and identity;

> » from a concern with generalising about learning processes in all learners to considering specific learners in specific times and places;

> » from a focus on schooling and formal education to other types of everyday contexts.

The professional learning theories in this book are mostly characterised by features from the latter part of these trajectories. They are concerned with the social learning of a variety of forms of knowledge and practice among specific groups in specific contexts that might not be formal education. The one possible exception is the reflective practice models considered in Chapter 2. In application, these models can lead to an emphasis on learning as an individual process without sufficient consideration of how social context and other shared forms of knowledge might influence, or be needed, in that learning. In addition, although Schön is interested in knowing-in-action, which can be a form of tacit knowledge, theories such as Kolb's experiential learning can be used to put too much emphasis on learning as explicit rational consideration of propositional knowledge and ignore tacit aspects of learning a professional practice.

It is worth noting that the move towards a concern with the social contexts of learning rather than individualistic, universal 'information processing' models can have contradictory expressions. For example, humanist theories of learning (such as Malcolm Knowles' work on andragogy) can emphasise the importance of individual learners' personal identities and biographies in what is learned, why and how. However, a sociocultural theory like Cultural Historical Activity Theory (CHAT) (Chapter 6) has been accused of ignoring personal differences and constructing all learners, in a specific cultural and historical context, as undifferentiated. Although humanist theories are not explicitly considered in this book, Hodkinson and Hodkinson's suggested revisions of communities of practice, reported in Chapter 5, are informed by similar concerns about individual learner biographies and their effects on what is learned rather than treating all learners as the same.

Individual or social context?

This difference between an emphasis on individual learners and an emphasis on social context is another key difference in the professional learning theories in this book. This has at least three related elements. To what extent do theories consider:

> » how experiences and knowledge need to be mentally worked on by individual learners in order for learning to happen?
> » the effects of social interactions or social organisation on learning?
> » how learners' personal differences affect what is learned, why and how?

Some theories focus on the mental work that individual learners are (or should be) doing in order to learn. Others focus on how the social context in which learning takes place influences learning. Eraut (Chapter 4) use a wave/particle analogy to try to avoid this dichotomy and to argue that learning is simultaneously individual and social. Eraut focuses both on the mental work individual learners need to develop professional competence and on how social conditions influence learning. However, other theories tend to foreground one over the other. CHAT and communities of practice emphasise social and community organisation and practices over either how individual learners 'process' their experiences or how individual learners' personal differences affect learning. Kolb and Schön seem to emphasise learning as individual 'information processing' without attention to the effects of specific contexts or to learner's personal differences (with the exception of Kolb's wider concern with different learning styles resulting from preferences for different stages of the learning cycle). Hodkinson and Hodkinson attempt to insert learners' personal differences into communities of practice but still focus mainly on social interaction and organisation rather than the work individual learners need to do with their experiences to learn.

How we learn or what we need to learn?

Another key difference in the professional learning theories in this book is between those that foreground how learning takes place (with either an individual or social focus) and those that foreground what it is that we need to learn. Experiential/reflective learning, CHAT and communities of practice foreground how learning takes place with little detailed consideration of the specifics of what we need to learn. Communities of practice argues that, as well as learning explicit knowledge, we also need to develop tacit knowledge and the identity, values and practices of the community. CHAT argues for expansive learning. Schön writes about knowledge-in-use and reflection-in-action. However, these are still relatively generic, which is not surprising given that these theories are not specific to particular professions. Pedagogical content knowledge (PCK) (Chapter 3), clinical practice (Chapter 7) and craft knowledge (Chapter 8) all foreground in specific detail what it is that needs to be learned in order to be a teacher. The best processes for learning this then follow from the nature of the knowledge, skills and dispositions that are needed. Eraut also gives some detailed consideration to what needs to be learned in professional (but not teaching-specific) learning as well as to the social organisation and experiences that best foster this.

Theory driven or empirically derived?

The final key difference that I am going to identify in this chapter, is the extent to which theories are built from empirical evidence or driven by the extension of theoretical models. This is a simplification of the relationship between these two things but, for heuristic purposes, it is a useful distinction. Perhaps the extreme ends of a continuum are CHAT and Eraut's research into workplace learning. The fundamental suppositions of CHAT are derived from an extension of Vygotsky's psychology, which in itself was influenced by Marx's theories. Although CHAT academic literature includes empirical data, this is mostly an exemplification or application of CHAT rather than data that gives rise to the theory. On the other hand, Eraut's models of the nature of professional knowledge and practice and the social interactions and organisation that support their development are generated (in part) from detailed empirical studies of actual workers/learners in actual organisations. So with CHAT (to simplify again) theory comes first and data comes afterwards, whereas for Eraut data comes first and theory comes afterwards. PCK and craft knowledge research centres on detailed empirical attempts to identify PCK and teacher's craft knowledge. However, Shulman's original postulation of PCK was not based on explicitly cited empirical evidence and, I would argue, that different models of PCK are based as much on normative judgments about what teachers should be doing as on evidence of actual teachers' professional knowledge. While early formulations of communities of practice give examples of communities of practice, these seem to have been gathered as much after the theory as before it.

It might seem that theories based on 'evidence' are preferable to those based on the elaboration or synthesis of other theories. However, in this context, theories derived from empirical observations could be accused of paying too much attention to the appearance of surface details and not enough to less visible factors that might be influential. As Marx wrote in *Capital*, if appearance and essence were the same thing there would be no need for any form of science.

IN A **NUTSHELL**

There are a number of 'dimensions' along which professional learning theories can differ. These include whether they:

» foreground individual learning processes or social interactions and social organisation;

» take account of personal differences in learners;

» foreground how learning happens or what needs to be learned;

» are generated from empirical evidence or from the elaboration or synthesis of other theories.

REFLECTIONS ON **CRITICAL ISSUES**

How valuable we find particular theories will depend on what it is we are trying to understand or improve when facilitating professional learning. In relation to communities of practice, Eraut questions whether the theory adds anything to our understanding of professional learning beyond what we could understand by empirical observation and research (see Chapter 5). On the other hand, Hughes, Jewson and Unwin (see Chapter 5) call communities of practice a paradigm shift, which suggests, in their view, that it certainly does add something, although they are also critical of some aspects of the theory.

In the introduction to this chapter I called theories of professional learning lenses that we could use to gain insights into the learning processes we want to facilitate. Perhaps this is the way to answer Eraut's question and to understand Hughes, Jewson and Unwin's idea of paradigm shift in relation to all of the theories of professional learning in this book. If they draw our attention to aspects of professional learning that we had not previously considered, and if acting on the insights we gain from this produces demonstrable improvements in our practice or outcomes, then they have proved useful. Even if we identify limitations with these theories, the questions they make us ask about those limitations might be different from the ones we would have asked before we encountered them.

CRITICAL **ISSUES**

- *How might these models help us understand professional learning?*
- *What are the limitations of these models?*
- *What might they mean for the organisation and processes of ITE (initial teacher education)?*

Introduction

This chapter considers some of the most influential theories of learning through reflection on experience that have been adopted, at various times, in Initial Teacher Education (ITE). These are Kolb's model of experiential learning (Kolb, 1983), Argyris and Schön's model of double loop learning (Argyris, 1976, 1999; Argyris and Schön, 1978) and Schön's ideas in relation to the reflective practitioner (Schön, 1990, 1994).

Kolb: experiential learning

Several experiential learning models conceptualise learning primarily as a cycle of reflection on experience. One of the best known of these models is Kolb's (1983) experiential learning cycle (Figure 2.1).

Kolb's model is often used to consider learning starting from the concrete experience stage but learning can start anywhere in the cycle. However, for the purposes of the discussion at this stage, we will consider the implications of the cycle if we *do* start with concrete experience. Using Kolb's model in this way our learning starts with a particular experience. After the experience we reflect on what happened and we use this reflection to build (or adapt) an understanding of the situation. We then use this understanding to plan our next actions and the cycle starts again.

This model of the learning process has some validity. However, it also has some limitations as a representation of professional learning or as a model for planning professional learning. Some of these limitations might result from inadequate understanding or applications of the model rather than from the original conceptualisation but they still need to be explored.

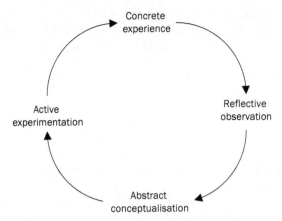

Figure 2.1 Kolb's experiential learning cycle.

One of these problems is the possible slippage of this model into a 'lone scientist' (to borrow a phrase from Piaget) conceptualisation of professional learning. 'Scientist' because this model apparently emphasises learning as a purely cognitive process of problem solving and knowledge building and has no obvious space for considering how other aspects such as values, affective factors and identity might influence the learning process. 'Lone' because it is possible to understand the model as one in which a solitary learner learns from their experience without sufficient explicit consideration of where the models or resources for the abstract conceptualisation stage of learning come from or whether they are shared and culturally situated rather than personal. The importance, for what and how we learn, of the particular sociocultural context in which we learn can be underemphasised in this model. It is perhaps significant that Kolb uses his model to create a typology of learners and that his work has been built on by others (eg Honey and Mumford, 1982) to create theories of individual learning styles. Arguably, this shows an emphasis on individual psychology in learning in this model and the relative neglect of sociocultural factors in learning.

Another possible limitation of this model is that it can lead to what some researchers on professional learning have called restrictive learning (Evans et al, 2006). Restrictive learning is perhaps best explained by an example. Using Kolb's experiential learning cycle as a model for understanding professional learning, it is possible to imagine a teacher who reflects on how to increase the test scores of their class. They could travel around the reflective learning cycle several times, each time getting better, on the basis of reflecting on experience at improving the test scores. However this learning might be restrictive because they never reflect on whether improving test scores is the most important thing to be doing or on whether improving test scores is a goal that should be achieved irrespective of the methods used. Restrictive learning can be thought of as getting better at achieving the goals defined by our work context, with the 'tools' we are given by that context, without considering whether these are the right goals or the appropriate tools.

Another related risk of restrictive learning for Kolb's model relates to situated rationality and situated cognition (Brown, Collins and Duguid, 1989). These ideas identify that the way in which we make sense of our experiences, and how we use our understanding to plan future action, depend on the particular ways of making sense or thinking about the world that are part of the culture of the institution that we are in. For Kolb's model this means that the process of abstract conceptualisation will occur through making sense of our individual experiences in terms of frameworks for understanding that are typically used in the institution in which we have the experiences.

If we accept this point, then the risk is that what we learn is limited by the models or ideas that are dominant in the context in which we are learning. This could mean that a student learning in one school could come to different conclusions about the same experience to those they would come to if they were learning in another. This is because they are using the ways of thinking and making sense that are typical or common in that school. This learning is restrictive because it does not recognise that the understanding of a situation in one institution is not universal but that different understandings of the same experience exist in different places.

A third possible problem with Kolb's model is related to the difficulty of producing paradigm shifts in people's thinking. Kolb's experiential learning cycle is based on the idea that our experiences will alter the ways we conceptualise the world. However, in many areas of intellectual life it has often been concluded that it takes a lot for experience to change our models of the world. In practice we tend to be very good at interpreting our experience to make it consistent with the models we already have. Some of the most influential versions of this view have been Kuhn's theory of paradigm shifts in science (Kuhn, 1996) in which much counter evidence is required before a prevailing paradigm will be abandoned in favour of a new one; Foucault's (2001) concept of the historical or disciplinary episteme that influences what is thought to be possible; and the idea of cognitive dissonance coined by Festinger (1957) in which we tend to explain away experiences that conflict with our dominant or cherished beliefs. A similar idea is captured in the notion of 'confirmation bias' in which we tend to emphasise aspects of experience that support our existing beliefs and downplay or ignore those that do not.

Argyris and Schön: double-loop learning

Some of the limitations of Kolb's model can be overcome adopting the double-loop learning model of Argyris and Schön (Argyris, 1976, 1999, Argyris and Schön, 1978). Argyris and Schön define single-loop learning as learning that takes place when the goals and frameworks of actions are taken for granted and we are just interested in how to operate more effectively within them. Double-loop learning takes place when we also reflect on the goals and frameworks such that learning may also involve changing these as well as changing how we operate within them.

The recognition that we need to go beyond the restrictive cycle of single-loop learning also acknowledges that what we learn might be socially and culturally situated and therefore limited by the world view of the particular institutions in which we operate. However, the main motivation for going beyond current institutionally specific ways of understanding a situation in the model of Argyris and Schön is the failure of the techniques currently being used to improve performance. It is this failure that prompts learners to examine the fundamental assumptions they are working within. If the techniques being used appear to be working to achieve the predefined goals of the institution we are in, we might not feel the need to question the value of the goals or the value of the techniques we are using. There is also still the problem of how difficult it is for our experiences to actually change the models we hold of the world rather than for our experience to be interpreted in terms of the models we already have.

Although values and emotions play a part in the double-loop learning model, other models of professional learning give a more central role to the ways in which these aspects influence what professional learning is and how it takes place. So this is an area that is still under-represented in this model.

Schön: the reflective practitioner

Perhaps the most famous name in relation to reflective learning and teacher education is Donald Schön, although most of his writing was not about teachers. It is largely because of Schön that the term 'reflective practitioner' became ubiquitous in teacher education. Schön is well known for writing about two types of reflection on practice: reflection-in-action and reflection-on-action (Schön, 1990, 1994). Reflection-in-action is Schön's term for the thinking we do, and the ways we adjust our actions, while in the middle of acting. An example is how teachers modify their approaches in a lesson during the lesson as a result of what is happening in the room. Reflection-on-action is similar to the reflective observation of Kolb's experiential learning cycle and happens after the event when we are thinking about what we might do in future.

Schön also wrote about the importance of framing and reframing problems (Schön, 1990, 1993). Framing is how we conceptualise or construct the problem; what sort of problem do we think it is? In some of his work Schön argues that how we frame a problem should receive as much attention as the solutions we suggest (Schön 1993). This is because how we construct problems will influence the types of solution we look for.

Another contribution that Schön made to understanding professional learning was to reject what he called 'technical rationality' in favour of the model of the reflective practitioner. Technical rationality is a view of knowledge that believes that there are stable and universal solutions to problems and that these can be applied across a range of contexts. A professional practitioner, therefore, just needs to take them 'off the peg' and apply them. As an alternative the reflective practice model emphasises the importance of personally generated, contextually specific solutions to ever-changing circumstances.

Personal practical knowledge

The last point leads us to consider the nature of teachers' knowledge and how this is related to what they have to learn and how they learn it. A technical rational model for teachers' learning would emphasise learning bodies of authoritative knowledge or theory first which we would then expect beginning teachers to apply to the specific circumstances of their practice. In an extreme version of this model, the teachers learning might be thought to be complete once they had mastered that body of knowledge. What happened in classrooms after that would be the application of knowledge. Occasionally, ITE students think this is how teacher education works or should work. They believe all of their professional learning will or should happen in the lecture theatre and seminar room before they go to the classroom and then they will apply what they have learned in the classroom. If they have to learn anything in the school they see this as a shortcoming of the course. However, a reflective practice-based model emphasises the centrality of the specific school and classroom as the key site for learning with teachers building their own understanding of practice by practising in that context.

Schön is not alone in emphasising the importance of personal practical knowledge (Clandinin and Connelly, 1995) generated by teachers through practice in specific contexts and comparing this favourably with authoritative knowledge that is generated outside of schools and is prescribed to schools as the right way of doing things. In recent years Connelly and Clandinin have written much about the central importance of teachers' personal practical knowledge in opposition to the rhetoric of conclusions (Clandinin and Connelly, 1995) generated by large-scale research and government policies. In part they base their work on the earlier critiques by Schwab (1958, 1969, 1971, 1973) on the dangers of narrow disciplinary theoretical knowledge and the superior value of teachers' practical knowledge.

However, whatever the undoubted value of knowledge generated by practitioners in schools there is still a risk of this being restrictive knowledge.

What are the implications of Kolb, Argyris and Schön's models of professional learning for the organisation and practices of ITE?

Reflecting on conceptualisation

I argued in the last section that Kolb's cycle of learning provides little detail on how our reflections on experience are formed into abstract conceptualisations. I would argue that they are largely fitted into ways of understanding the world that are easily available to us as cultural tools or resources. There are a number of readymade ways of understanding the world in any given culture that can be used for making sense of the experiences we have. When students are new to ITE it is likely that the cultural resources they use for making sense of their experience will be those available in the wider world outside of the specific context in which they are learning. They might draw on media representations of education and young people. Equally they might draw on the understanding of school they acquired when they were at school themselves. Or they might draw on what Bruner has called 'folk psychology' – general, non-specialist ways of understanding or explaining human behaviour that are prevalent within any culture (Bruner, 1990).

As they gain experience in a particular school, it is increasingly likely that students will use the ways of making sense of teaching and learning that are common in that school or department. Their abstract conceptualisation will come from the ways that things are routinely conceptualised by the people they work with. However, there are risks that this will become restrictive learning or single-loop learning. Although, they may become increasingly proficient at fitting in with the expectations of their host school, what is needed from a process of teacher education is expansive learning (Evans et al, 2006); this is the ability to see beyond the world view and practices of any single school or department at any moment in time.

One way to minimise this risk is to pay explicit and careful attention to the abstract conceptualisation part of the learning cycle. In practice the process of conceptualisation can be largely implicit or hidden. Students develop ways of understanding their experience through their interaction with more experienced members of the school but they rarely expose this conceptualisation to explicit examination. One way to minimise the risk of restrictive learning within this understanding of the learning process is to ensure that learners are provided explicitly with more than one way of understanding their experiences. This means offering alternative theories or models for experience and subjecting initial conceptualisations of experience to critical scrutiny. Alternative models can come from educational research and theory or from considering how different people make different sense of the same experience.

Theory and practice relationships

The provision of alternative models for understanding experiences raises another consideration. In the first section I commented that Kolb's cycle is often used as if the process of learning always starts from experience. However, the learning process can start anywhere in the cycle. One of the possible limitations of traditional ITE courses is that they typically start the learning cycle with abstract conceptualisation. Teaching students are introduced to educational research and theories in a generalised relatively abstracted form first and are then expected to apply them to specific situations of practice. Viewed unsympathetically, this can look like a technical-rationalist approach to ITE in which teacher learning consists of acquiring a body of knowledge and skills that can then be applied to diverse situations of practice. However, this characterisation would not be entirely fair as most traditional ITE courses have built into them the expectation that students will reflect on their practice and use this to modify and adapt approaches to teaching and learning. Nevertheless, problems still remain with starting the learning cycle with abstract conceptualisation. Many students find it difficult to understand how to relate the abstract conceptualisations to the specific experiences they have. This often leads to them considering the theories and practices they learned in the university as irrelevant and they often seek alternative ways of understanding experience through the sense-making resources (that is ideas, beliefs, practices) routinely used in the school (for example, see Philpott, 2006).

What this consideration leads to is the need to recognise the difficulties of starting student learning with an input of research or theory or specific strategies. This is not uniquely a problem of university-based ITE; it can also be duplicated as a practice in school-based training programmes and in the CPD events that more experienced teachers attend. In these situations, learners are presented with a theory or a strategy first and are then expected to take it away and use it. Again, this runs the risk of becoming a technical-rationalist approach. A better model is to use theories or models after students have had experiences in order to encourage them to conceptualise their experiences in different ways and to reflect on the relative merits of different conceptualisations. This is more like Argyris and Schön's double-loop learning model in which we are invited to reflect on the value of our current assumptions and goals as well as on how to improve our practice within them. It also has a useful similarity to Billet's idea of 'disembedding' in professional education (Billett, 1996, 1998). This is the idea that we should learn by moving from considering a collection of specific experiences in specific contexts to a more generalised, transferrable understanding of those experiences rather than starting with generalisations and trying to apply those to the specific contexts of practice.

Supply-side and demand-side learning

Another consideration relevant to where we start in the experiential learning cycle and, therefore, how we sequence practical experiences and abstracted models, comes from Brown and Duguid's (2000) distinction between 'supply-side' and 'demand-side' learning. Brown and Duguid argue that much formal education is supply-side learning. What is learned, how and when, is decided by the providers of the learning rather than the learners. Therefore, it might not be related to the particular concerns or curiosity of the learner at that point in their learning. However, demand-side learning is led by learners who learn what they want to learn, how and when they want to learn it. The assumption is that demand-side learning is more effective as it relates to what learners want to know, when they want to know it. A risk of supply-side learning is that learners cannot assimilate the things they are expected to learn in relation to what they already understand.

Starting the experiential learning cycle with abstract conceptualisation could be seen as a form of supply-side learning as it could be that student teachers are being asked to make sense of ideas and models that do not yet relate to any experiences they have had. Using abstract conceptualisation retrospectively to make sense of experiences learners have had, and, perhaps more importantly, challenges they are wrestling with, is more like demand-side learning. Effectively, learners are asking what they need to know to make a success of the situation they currently find themselves in.

Learning reflection in action

One particular consideration arising from what reflective models of learning tell us about effective support for school-based learning in ITE comes from considering Schön's reflection-in-action. This refers to the way in which skilled practitioners reflect on what they are doing and modify it while they are doing it. This is a skill of experienced teachers that might not be visible to student teachers. The development of this ability can be supported by making it more visible. One way of achieving this is for experienced teachers to talk through the decisions they made during the lesson and why after they have been observed by a student teacher.

IN A **NUTSHELL**

Although reflective practice models such as those of Kolb, Argyris and Schön have historically been very influential on teacher education, they are arguably over reliant on considering learners as decontextualised individuals and on considering reflection as a rational cognitive process. Conversely, they do not pay enough attention to the social aspects of professional learning and the non-cognitive or rational aspects of learning.

REFLECTIONS ON **CRITICAL ISSUES**

Models of learning through reflection on experience help us to understand that transmission models of professional learning or technical rational models have severe limitations. They help us to see that an important part of learning to practice comes through engagement with experience rather than happening before it. They also help us to see the value of the personal practical knowledge that practitioners have compared to the abstract codified knowledge of theory and, sometimes, government policies.

Their limitations are that they do not take enough account of the ways in which sociocultural context shapes and perhaps limits what we learn. They also do not take enough account of the role that identity, values and emotions play in how we learn or how difficult it can be for experience to actually change the ways we fundamentally conceptualise the world.

Reflective models of learning help us see that the way in which ITE is organised should take account of the amount of learning that is needed, and that takes place, after experience rather than before it. This post-experiential learning needs to be given proper consideration and support and not just left to chance. Post-experiential learning also needs to take account of the ways in which there might be more than one way of making sense of experience.

Further reading

Argyris, C (1999) *Organisational Learning*. London: Wiley Blackwell.

Kolb, D A (1983) *Experiential Learning: Experience as the Source of Learning and Development*. London: Prentice Hall.

Schön, D A (1990) *Educating the Reflective Practitioner: Toward a New Design for Teaching and Learning in the Professions*. London: Wiley.

Schön, D A (1993) Generative Metaphor, in Ortony, A (ed) *Metaphor and Thought*. Cambridge: Cambridge University Press.

> ## CRITICAL **ISSUES**
>
> - *What is pedagogical content knowledge (PCK)?*
> - *How can we identify what PCK is?*
> - *How is PCK developed?*
> - *What implications does PCK have for ITE?*

Introduction

The idea of pedagogical content knowledge (PCK) in its current form(s) was first proposed by Shulman (1986, 1987). However, Bullough (2001) argues that it is the revival of an earlier idea, and Ball (2000) draws connections between PCK and some of Dewey's much earlier arguments on the nature of teacher knowledge and teacher education. PCK is the knowledge that teachers have that non-teachers do not. It is the difference between what a teacher of a subject knows and what another graduate in the subject knows. Identifying what PCK is and where it comes from can serve as the foundation for teacher education as it sets the destination for the teacher education process and the route for getting there (Abell, 2008).

Bullough (2001) argues that interest in PCK grew because of political concerns about teacher professionalism and quality, and concerns about the status and impact of teacher education. In the early twentieth century, Bullough argues, positing PCK was part of an attempt to bolster the status of teacher education in relation to more traditional higher education disciplines. Similarly, interest in PCK in the late twentieth century can be linked to concerns about the need for formal programmes of teacher education, the impact of programmes on teacher quality and the status of teaching as a profession.

What is PCK?

The simple account

In its simplest form PCK can be understood as an amalgam of disciplinary content knowledge and pedagogical knowledge. Shulman (1986, 1987) argues that there has been a tendency to separate these, both conceptually in research on teaching and in practice in teacher education. Knowledge of pedagogy has been seen to be content neutral, with general pedagogical principles being researched and advocated. Similarly, developing disciplinary content knowledge has been seen as a process separate from pedagogy.

In undergraduate courses of ITE this might mean that developing subject expertise and developing pedagogical expertise are done in separate modules. In postgraduate (secondary) ITE this might mean that the development of subject knowledge is seen as having been completed at undergraduate level with ITE focusing on the development of pedagogical knowledge.

The PCK argument is that teachers' pedagogical understanding transforms (Gess-Newsome, 1999) their subject knowledge. This transformation enables different representations of the subject depending on pedagogical need (Shulman, 1986, 1987; Van Driel, Verloop and de Vos, 1998; Ball and Bass, 2000). So a teacher does not have the same subject knowledge as another graduate with the addition of pedagogical knowledge; they have PCK in which pedagogical knowledge and subject knowledge have transformed into an indivisible new form of knowledge

However, over 20 years after this *'seductive'* (Van Driel, Veal and Janssen, 2001,p 984) argument was put forward, PCK is still regarded as *'slippery'* (Van Driel, Veal and Janssen, 2001, p 984) and *'elusive'* (Van Driel, Veal and Janssen, 2001, p 984; Ball 2000, p 241), subject to *'conceptual confusion'* (Van Driel, Veal and Janssen, 2001, p 982) and *'inconsistent'* and *'vague'* in application (Abell, 2008, p 1407). Abell (2008, p 1413) concludes that *'We still do not know enough about what PCK ... teachers have, how they come to have it, or what they do with it'*.

The not-so-simple account

One reason PCK has proved elusive is because it has been defined differently by different proponents. The idea that PCK involves an amalgamation of subject knowledge and pedagogical knowledge is shared by most proponents (Van Driel and Berry, 2010). However, other factors that might contribute to PCK, and the relationship between these, are seen differently. Shulman (1986, pp 9–10) initially identified three categories of teacher knowledge:

1. subject matter content knowledge – knowledge of the subject, its organisation and practices;

2. pedagogical content knowledge – a form of knowing the subject organised according to its *'teachability'* (p 9);

3. curricular knowledge – knowledge of the resources and methods that could be used for teaching the subject.

Later Shulman (1987, p 8) expanded these three categories into seven:

1. content knowledge;

2. general pedagogical knowledge, with special reference to those broad principles and strategies of classroom management and organization that appear to transcend subject matter;

3. curriculum knowledge, with particular grasp of the materials and programs that serve as *'tools of the trade'* for teachers;

15

4. pedagogical content knowledge, that special amalgam of content and pedagogy that is uniquely the province of teachers, their own special form of professional understanding;

5. knowledge of learners and their characteristics;

6. knowledge of educational contexts, ranging from the workings of the group or classroom, the governance and financing of school districts, to the character of communities and cultures; and

7. knowledge of educational ends, purposes, and values, and their philosophical and historical grounds.

PCK (category 4 on the list above) has a different relationship to the other categories on the list. It is at least an amalgam of content knowledge and general pedagogical knowledge. However, Shulman also suggests that PCK involves knowledge of learners and their characteristics. This is both generalised characteristics and characteristics of specific learners (Shulman, 1986, 1987). PCK can also include values (part of category 7) (Gudmundsdottir and Shulman, 1987; Gudmundsdottir, 1990; Zembylas, 2007). So we can question what constitutes PCK, as well as how PCK relates to other categories in the teachers' knowledge base (Abell, 2008).

Carlsen (1999) sets out some differences between different conceptions of PCK including three that are 'seminal' (p 136) (Table 3.1). The black areas indicate a major category in the model, grey areas indicate a subsidiary category and white areas indicate something that is not explicitly referenced.

Table 3.1 Domains of teacher knowledge: four alternatives from Carlsen, 1999.

Knowledge category or domain	Shulman, 1986	Shulman and Sykes, 1986	Shulman, 1987	Grossman, 1990
Curriculum	▨	■	□	▨
Learners and learning	□	■	■	▨
Liberal knowledge and skills (general)	□	■	□	□
Pedagogy (general)	□	■	■	■
Pedagogical content knowledge	▨	■	■	■
Performance skills	□	■	□	■
Philosophy, goals, objectives	□	■	■	▨
School contexts	□	■	■	■
Subject matter (content)	■	■	■	■
Substantive structures of the discipline	▨	□	□	▨
Syntactic structures of the discipline	▨	□	□	▨

Kind (2009) compares nine different models (Table 3.2, see overleaf). P indicates that a category forms part of PCK, K indicates that it forms part of the teachers' knowledge base but is separate from PCK and 0 indicates that the category is not explicitly discussed.

Table 3.2 shows that the number of models has proliferated and so has the number of possible categories for inclusion in PCK. It also shows differences of opinion about what forms part of PCK and what is in the teachers' knowledge base but outside of PCK.

Different views about composition are part of the explanation for why identifying PCK has proved elusive in practice. A second reason, discussed in the next section, relates to a tension between the theoretical and the empirical aspects of the PCK project.

(How) can we identify what PCK is?

Empirical and theoretical tensions

Shulman (1986, 1987) originally posited PCK as a model of teacher knowledge but did not provide any empirical evidence of its existence or its nature. However, he did initiate a programme of empirical research into the nature of PCK. This research has used a number of approaches for trying to elicit teachers' PCK and compare it with that of less experienced teachers or teachers without formal training (Grossman, 1989). Kind (2009) includes a good overview of the research approaches that have been used.

However, there is a tension in this enterprise between its empirical and theoretical aspects. Consider the nine models of PCK in Table 3.2. How many of the categories in these models are derived from empirical evidence and how many are included because researchers believe they *should* be included in a model of teacher knowledge? Consider '*socio-cultural aspects*' in Veal and MaKinster's (1999) model. Is this included because they have identified it empirically or is it there because they think that good teachers should take this into account? If the former, why are they the only researchers to find it? If PCK is something more than idiosyncratic, then surely the categories that contribute to it should be consistent across teachers? If it is not consistent, can it form the basis of a goal for teacher education? Perhaps other researchers have subsumed socio-cultural aspects under another category. However, this does not remove the fundamental issue.

At the inception of PCK, Shulman offers a vision of the knowledge base he thinks a good teacher should be using rather than evidence of what teachers are actually using (Shulman, 1986, 1987). Even the idea of PCK as a transformative rather than an integrative model (Gess-Newsome, 1999) is a normative vision (see for example, Cochran, King and DeRuiter, 1991) rather than one based on empirical evidence. Lederman and Gess-Newsome (1992) use the analogy of the ideal gas law to suggest that PCK might be true in an ideal circumstance rather than in the specific contexts of particular teachers and classrooms.

Table 3.2 Some different models of PCK adapted from Kind, 2009.

Authors	Representations and instructional strategies	Students' subject specific learning difficulties	Purposes/ orientations/ nature of subject	Curricular knowledge	Subject matter knowledge	Context for learning	General pedagogy/ classroom management	Assessment	Socio-cultural issues	School knowledge
Shulman (1987)	P	P	K	K	K	K	K	O	O	O
Grossman (1980)	P	P	P	P	K	K	K	O	O	O
Magnusson, Krajcik and Borko (1999)	P	P	P	P	K	K	K	P	O	O
Marks (1990)	P	P	O	P	P	O	O	O	O	O
Fernandez-Balboa and Stiehl (1995)	P	P	P	O	P	P	O	O	O	O
Koball, Graber, Colewman and Kemp (1999)	O	P	O	P	P	P	P	O	O	O
Cochran, deRuiter and King (1993)	O	P	O	O	P	P	P	O	O	O
Veal and MaKinster (1999)	P	P	P	P	P	P	P	P	P	O
Banks, Leach and Moon (2005)	O	O	O	O	P	O	P	O	O	P

Whose PCK should we research?

This tension is further emphasised by questions about which teachers to research to identify PCK empirically (Abell, 2008). Not all experienced teachers have the PCK that we are interested in developing in beginning teachers (Loughran, Berry and Mulhall, 2006; Abell, 2008). In trying to identify PCK empirically do we study all teachers? Do we study only 'good' teachers? If so, how do we identify them? Is it those with good test scores? Is it those that fit the researchers' normative model of what a good teacher does? There are possible ways out of this uncertainty. Shulman suggests that teacher communities know who good teachers are and Millican (2013) adopts a similar approach by using *'social interaction analysis'* (p 47) to canvass teachers' opinions about who is good. However, there are questions inherent in this approach too.

How generalisable is PCK?

The empirical approach to identifying PCK has other challenges. One of the premises of PCK is that it is subject and topic specific. Although there is speculation about a broader version of PCK or shared elements in PCK that might allow us to identify generic PCK (Fernandez-Balboa and Stiehl, 1995) or PCK for a subject or broad areas within a subject (Abell, 2008), much PCK research has focused on narrow topic areas (eg De Jong, Van Driel and Verloop, 2005; Drechsler and Van Driel, 2008; Henze, Van Driel and Verloop, 2008). Shulman's original model, and later models and research, also indicate that PCK can be context specific, related to particular schools and pupils. It can also be teacher specific as teachers' values and orientation towards the subject can influence the nature of PCK. Some research suggests that even where many of these things are consistent across teachers, individual teacher PCK can still be different (Loughran, Berry and Mulhall, 2006; Van Driel, Verloop and de Vos, 1998; Van Driel and Berrry, 2012). Loughran, Berry and Mulhall (2006) argue that, even where they have identified several different versions of PCK in relation to a specific topic for several teachers, this does not represent all the possibilities and that there may be other forms of PCK in relation to these topics that are equally effective.

So does this mean that PCK is personal and idiosyncratic? Individuals might have an identifiable PCK that is different from non-teachers or untrained teachers. However, unless we can identify something common, can we use the idea of PCK to inform teacher education? (Van Driel, Verloop and de Vos, 1998). Perhaps all we can generalise from empirical evidence is that skilled teachers reconfigure their subject knowledge in ways that take account of pupils, context, values, educational purposes, their own conception of the subject, assessment and any other thing that we think we should add. This would suggest that PCK research has not moved us on from the initial statement of the idea over 20 years ago, with the exception of adding more categories that not everyone agrees with.

Some researchers have developed ways of addressing this apparent difficulty. Loughran, Berry and Mulhall (2006) gather multiple versions of PCK in relation to specific topics and offer these to teachers for consideration in developing their own PCK. Using a different approach Van Driel, Verloop and de Vos (1998) synthesise individual teacher variations in PCK into a single model. However, the number of factors that can influence PCK and the variations in identified PCK even where these factors are similar is another reason why PCK has proved elusive in practice.

Why is so much PCK research in science and mathematics?

Some of the earliest PCK research is in relation to English (Grossman, 1989; Gudmundsdottir, 1991) and social science (Gudmundsdottir and Shulman, 1987; Gudmundsdottir, 1990). Although there continue to be examples of PCK research in music (Haston and Leon-Guerrero, 2008; Millican, 2013), literacy (Phelps and Schilling, 2004), second-language learning (Liu, 2013; Sanchez and Borg, 2014) history, (Monte-Sano, 2011), geography (Ormrod and Cole, 1996) and PE (Ayvazo and Ward, 2011), these are isolated examples compared to the volume of work in science and mathematics. Why should PCK not have taken hold equally in all subject areas?

Shulman's original articulation of PCK posits an amalgamation of subject knowledge and pedagogical knowledge. It also acknowledges the influence of other factors such as context, individual pupils, and educational values. Part of the amalgamation of subject knowledge and pedagogical knowledge relates to understanding pupils' common difficulties with particular topics including common conceptions and misconceptions. This is an area that has been extensively researched in science and mathematics. PCK research in science and mathematics education tends to emphasise common conceptions and misconceptions as a central feature of PCK (eg Van Driel, Verloop and de Vos, 1998; Ball and Bass, 2000). Sometimes it seems to reduce PCK to an amalgam of subject knowledge and knowledge of common conceptions and misconceptions. Although other factors are mentioned, these get left in the margins.

The usefulness of this for the PCK project is that this approach has more chance of producing generalisable models of PCK. If we bracket off factors like personal educational values, sociocultural differences, individual pupil biographies, teacher biographies, school differences and focus on relatively predictable issues like common conceptions and misconceptions about specific topics, we are more likely to produce examples of PCK that are transferrable.

In contrast there is little research on common conceptions and misconceptions in the arts and humanities. This is because the idea of common (cognitive) misconceptions does not make the same sense in these areas. Difficulties in arts and humanities learning in schools are often related to attitude, affect and personal factors rather than to cognitive misconceptions. So 'Shakespeare is boring' is a (predictable) pupil conception that teachers have to overcome, but how we overcome it will vary on the basis of sociocultural and personal factors related to both teachers and pupils. These are more variable than the cognitive misconceptions of science and mathematics.

Early PCK research on English (Grossman, 1989; Gudmundsdottir, 1991) and social sciences (Gudmundsdottir and Shulman, 1987; Gudmundsdottir, 1990) gives more prominence to personal orientations towards subject and values. As a result it also becomes more specific to individual teachers. The recent isolated examples of PCK research in the arts and humanities focus on technical aspects of the subject such as understanding phonemes in spelling (Phelps and Schilling, 2004) and correct embouchure and posture in instrumental tuition (Millican, 2013). These are areas in which difficulties and solution are more likely to transcend sociocultural and personal factors. If we want to build a picture of transferrable PCK that can be used to inform teacher education, it may be that this enterprise is more achievable in some subjects than others.

How does PCK develop and what are the implications for ITE?

The development of PCK

The most important factor identified in the development of PCK is teaching experience (Van Driel, Verloop and de Vos, 1998; Van Driel and De Jong, 2001). Although experience is necessary to develop PCK, it is not sufficient. This is true of experienced teachers who may not have developed PCK in a form that is considered desirable (Loughran, Berry and Mulhall, 2006; Abell, 2008). It is also true for student teachers. Grossman (1989) argues that English graduates teaching without formal teacher education interpreted their experiences inadequately compared to those with formal teacher education. So PCK had developed through experience with differing degrees of success. This suggests that it is the interaction between experience and formal study of education that develops appropriate PCK. This is unsurprising because it was envisaged in Shulman's original model.

How can we develop PCK most effectively?

Research suggests that the development of PCK is not linear and that it is unpredictable, so there is no simple recipe for ensuring its development (Van Driel, Verloop and de Vos, 1998; Magnusson, Krajcik and Borko, 1999; Veal, Tippins and Bell, 1999; Van Driel and Berry, 2012). However, there is agreement on what is helpful in the design of teacher education.

There is agreement that teaching experience alone is not sufficient for developing PCK. Experience needs to interact with forms of codified knowledge and normative perspectives on education of the type that result from the formal study of education (Van Driel, Verloop and de Vos, 1998).

Secondly, the separation of subject knowledge and pedagogy is a problem. PCK involves reconstructing the way in which teachers understand their subject. When considering pedagogy, we have to consider it in relation to specific content and consider how the demands of teaching require us to reconfigure our understanding of the topic being taught.

For undergraduate courses of teacher education this means avoiding a separation of subject and pedagogy. For postgraduate teacher education it means revisiting subject knowledge and thinking about reconfiguration rather than tacking pedagogy as a tool box onto existing subject knowledge. In general terms anything that separates subject knowledge from pedagogy hinders the development of PCK. Also, lack of attention to the nature of student teachers' subject knowledge can be a problem. Some PCK problems can arise from students' own lack of deep understanding of the areas they are teaching or their inability to rethink them in multiple ways that differ from how they were taught them.

Where subject knowledge is being developed as an aspect of ITE, this should be done in the context of specific learners and classrooms so that subject knowledge is configured in the context of pupil understanding from the outset (Cochran, DeRuiter and King, 1993). This could mean learning an area of subject knowledge by using case study materials to consider how specific pupils understand it.

Thirdly, there is agreement that making the idea of PCK explicit in teacher education helps. Students, tutors and mentors need to understand the idea of PCK and understand that this is what they are trying to develop (Abell, 2008; Loughran, Mulhall and Berry, 2008; Kind, 2009; Nilsson and Loughran, 2012). This can also help mentors and students understand what the tacit knowledge of mentors might be and where it might be found (Loughran, Mulhall and Berry, 2008).

Knowledge or process?

Much recent PCK research has tried to identify PCK in relation to specific topics. However, perhaps there is something problematic about the idea of PCK as a body of knowledge. Cochran, DeRuiter and King (1993) choose to refine the term PCK to PCKg – pedagogical content *knowing*. This emphasises it as an action rather than a piece of knowledge. Mason (1999) also emphasises PCK as an *ability* to combine subject knowledge with pedagogical knowledge rather than as a body of knowledge. So teacher education should perhaps develop the ability to think in terms of PCK rather than as transmitting a bank of topic-specific PCK.

There is a further problem for viewing PCK as a body of knowledge. PCK is topic and learner specific. PCK as a complete body of knowledge would be large. It would also be vulnerable to changes in school curriculum. This conception of PCK also runs counter to prevailing trends in teacher education which emphasise equipping student teachers with the skills to generate understanding of practice rather than providing readymade answers. For this reason it may be best to embed the process of thinking about the nature and importance of PCK and the process of developing it in relation to specific topics and learners rather than trying to build a bank of PCK as knowledge.

Individual or collective?

Another conception of PCK is offered by McNicholl, Child and Burn (2013) who suggest that it might be distributed within groups of teachers and also distributed through artefacts like resources as much as held in the heads of individual teachers. This collective nature of PCK is also raised by Abell (2008). This shifts the attention of ITE to fostering beginning teachers' abilities to develop, share and appraise collective PCK embodied in artefacts.

IN A **NUTSHELL**

It is important that we can identify what teachers' professional knowledge is and that we can enhance the focus and impact of ITE in relation to this. We need to work in purposeful and informed rather than haphazard ways. The political imperatives that gave rise to interest in PCK are still with us and PCK might still offer a way forward. An idea whose time seems to have come – clinical practice models (see Chapter 7) – often cites the work of researchers in PCK as part of its evidence base. This suggests that although PCK may so far have proved elusive, it is still relevant.

Identifying what teachers are thinking while practising is worthwhile. It is also helpful to recognise that how we understand a teaching subject is important and needs to be a part of teacher education. Even if different teachers do it differently, the fact that they are rethinking the subject in ways that make it teachable is a valuable insight into what ITE is trying to achieve.

REFLECTIONS ON **CRITICAL ISSUES**

Pedagogical content knowledge is the knowledge skilled teachers have that allows them to understand their subject in ways that make it teachable. Attempts to identify specific examples of PCK have been hindered by different models and by the specificity of particular examples of PCK. It is an idea that has taken hold more in research in science and mathematics than it has across the full range of school subjects. PCK develops mostly through practical experience but it needs to be informed by perspectives and knowledge from the formal study of education. One of the main implications for ITE is that paying continuing attention to the quality and nature of subject knowledge and its relationship to pedagogy is important.

Further reading

Abell, S K (2008) Twenty Years Later: Does Pedagogical Content Knowledge Remain a Useful Idea? *International Journal of Science Education*, 30(10): 1405–16.

Kind, V (2009) Potential Content Knowledge in Science Education: Perspectives and Potential for Progress. *Studies in Science Education*, 45(2): 169–204.

Shulman, L S (1987) Knowledge and Teaching: Foundations of the New Reform. *Harvard Educational Review*, 57(1): 1–22.

CRITICAL **ISSUES**

- *What is the nature of professional knowledge?*
- *How do we develop professional knowledge?*
- *What does the work of Michael Eraut add to our understanding?*

Introduction

This chapter considers the contribution of research on workplace learning to understanding the nature of professional knowledge and learning in teacher education. Workplace learning has been widely researched. However, until relatively recently, much of this research has not impacted widely on teacher education (Murray, McNamara and Jones, 2014). A possible exception to this is the work of Michael Eraut, which gained some popularity in teacher education, perhaps due to Eraut's own work in the area (eg Eraut, 2000a).

Eraut is a key researcher in how professionals learn in workplace settings. His contribution to understanding professional knowledge and learning is perhaps more clearly based on detailed empirical observation of actual learners in actual workplace settings than some other models of professional learning (for example, Cultural Historical Activity Theory and, according to Eraut (2002), Communities of Practice). Eraut has also shown an interest in analysing key concepts in professional knowledge and learning, such as tacit knowledge and reflection, that he claims others have taken for granted or failed to be sufficiently precise about. In general, Eraut has been concerned not to oversimplify the composition of professional knowledge or the processes that lead to its development but to capture them in all their detail, nuance and complexity. The result of this is that his work often involves breaking down ideas into their constituent parts and considering the relationships between those parts and also between those parts and other features of the situation. As a result, it might sometimes seem that Eraut's work identifies more challenges than it supplies solutions. However, he does offer guidance on the conditions that support effective professional learning.

What is professional knowledge?

Eraut rejects a dichotomy between knowledge as personal or knowledge as social (Eraut, 2010). He criticizes experiential learning models (for example, Kolb, 1983) for taking insufficient account of the social dimension of learning and knowledge, and models such as communities of practice for taking insufficient account of the personal. He uses the analogy of wave and particle theories of light to suggest that knowledge is both personal and social. Knowledge is socially constructed and acquired but we also need to attend to the ways in which individual trajectories through different social contexts affect how individuals learn and what they know.

Eraut (2010) argues that thinking about knowledge has traditionally focused on codified knowledge. This is the form of knowledge that is found in books, examinations and formal education in general. It is also the form of knowledge that is stored in the semantic memory and that can usually be recalled explicitly (Eraut, 2000b, 2004).

In addition to codified knowledge, Eraut identifies that performance in the workplace also depends on uncodified or cultural knowledge. Much of this is acquired through implicit and informal learning through participation in the workplace. As a result it may also be tacit knowledge. Although we can use it, we cannot necessarily call it explicitly to mind and articulate it. Cultural or uncodified knowledge is more likely to be stored in the episodic memory which stores our personal experiences (Eraut, 2000b, 2004). We tend to think about codified knowledge in terms of truth or falsity. We tend to think about cultural or uncodified knowledge in terms of its useability and who uses it and where.

Eraut defines personal knowledge as 'what individual persons bring to situations that enable them to think, interact and perform' (inter alia Eraut and Hirsh, 2007, p 6). The truth value of personal knowledge is less important than its use value. He identifies what personal knowledge is by providing a list of its component parts. In most of his work this list is:

» codified knowledge in the form(s) in which a person uses it;

» knowhow in the forms of skills and practices;

» personal understandings of people and situations;

» accumulated memories of cases and episodic events;

» other aspects of personal expertise, practical wisdom and tacit knowledge;

» self-knowledge, attitudes, values and emotions.

However, in its most recent version Eraut (2014, p 48) lists personal knowledge as:

» codified knowledge ready for use;

» knowledge acquired through enculturation;

» knowledge constructed from experience, social interaction and reflection;

» skills developed through practice with feedback;

» episodes, impressions and images that provide the foundations for informal knowledge;

» self-knowledge, attitudes, value and emotions.

This is not a fundamentally different list but it does suggest some refinement in the expression of the key components.

In practice, Eraut argues, the knowledge that he has analysed into component parts works in an integrated way. The advantage of much implicitly learned tacit knowledge is that it is already accessible in an integrated ready-to-use form in the context in which it was learned. This is less true of codified knowledge that may have been learned somewhere else. Eraut lists codified knowledge, above, in relation to *use* because in order for codified knowledge to be part of what enables people to think, interact and perform, it needs to be accessible in a form that is useable in a particular situation. We may know how to use codified knowledge in the situation in which it was acquired, that is formal education, but be less sure how to use it in another practice context. This is a problem of transfer of learning across contexts that can affect uncodified knowledge as much as codified. This brings us to the next question.

How do we use knowledge in professional contexts?

Eraut uses the term 'performance' in relation to professional practice, which includes the actions taken during the 'performance period' and those taken in preparation for it and reflection on it afterwards (Eraut, 2004). Professional performance has four elements that can be analytically separated but that in practice are interconnected and possibly recursive:

1. assessing clients and situations (sometimes briefly, sometimes involving a long process of investigation), and continuing to monitor them;

2. deciding what, if any, action to take, both immediately and over a longer period (either individually or as a member of a team);

3. pursuing an agreed course of action, modifying, consulting and reassessing as and when necessary;

4. meta-cognitive monitoring by individuals or collective monitoring within groups of the people involved, where agents or clients, and the general progress of the problem, project or situation.

The nature of this process is affected by the context in which it takes place and also by the perceived timescale that a practitioner has to evaluate and act. Eraut creates a tabular representation of the interaction between the timescale of practice and the effect this has on the 'mode of cognition' of professional practice (Table 4.1).

This relationship can be understood in two ways. Firstly, when we feel under the pressure of time we have to react in more rapid, intuitive and routinised ways. Secondly, as we become more proficient as practitioners we can react more rapidly and intuitively even where pressure of time does not demand it.

Table 4.1 Interactions between time, mode of cognition and process (from Eraut, 2007).

Type of process	Mode of cognition		
	Instant/reflex	Rapid/intuitive	Deliberative/analytic
Assessment of the situation	Pattern recognition	Rapid interpretation Communication on the spot	Prolonged diagnosis Review, discussion and analysis
Decision making	Instant response	Recognition primed or intuitive	Deliberative analysis or discussion
Overt actions	Routinised actions	Routines punctuated by rapid decisions	Planned actions with periodic progress reviews
Metacognitive engagement	Situational awareness	Implicit monitoring Short, reactive reflections	Monitoring of thought and activity, reflective learning Group evaluation

Rapid responses depend on professional knowledge that is 'ready for use' in the situation we are in and this can favour tacit cultural knowledge over codified or deliberative knowledge. Eraut claims that the nature of these situations mean that personal understanding of a situation (based on episodic memory) takes priority over other forms of knowledge. In fact, one thing that distinguishes experts from novices is less the total amount of knowledge they have than their proficiency at reading or recognising a situation based on episodic memory.

One consequence of this relationship is that in instant/reflex or rapid/intuitive situations inexperienced practitioners (and sometimes experienced ones) will draw on pattern recognition and routinised actions even if they are less appropriate than other responses. In the case of novice teachers, for example, this can mean reverting to patterns that they remember from their own days as pupils or those that they have observed elsewhere.

This point leads to a consideration of how we use the knowledge we already have to respond to professional situations and this is an issue of knowledge transfer.

Transfer of knowledge in professional contexts

Eraut (2004b) outlines transfer of knowledge as a series of steps:

1. the extraction of potentially relevant knowledge from the context(s) of its acquisition and previous use;

2. understanding the new situation, a process that often depends on informal social learning;

3. recognizing what knowledge and skills are relevant;

4. transforming them to fit the new situation;

5. integrating them with other knowledge and skills in order to think/act/communicate in the new situation.

In general terms, Eraut argues, the amount of work involved in transferring knowledge from one situation to another is unacknowledged or neglected. This is particularly true, he suggests, of academic/workplace partnerships where cultures of knowledge, its acquisition and use are very different and where neither side either recognises or takes responsibility for the work that is needed to transfer knowledge (mostly steps 4 and 5). The end result is that all parties (academia, workplace and student/worker) feel dissatisfied.

As suggested in the last section, practice contexts will tend to draw more easily on ready-to-use integrated knowledge that has been learned implicitly in the same context. In general terms, the more similar the context of use to the context of acquisition, the more readily knowledge will transfer. However, this does not mean it is necessarily the best knowledge or practice for the situation, and it can lead to an unhelpful conservatism.

In some of his earlier work (Eraut, 1985, 1994) Eraut sets out 'modes of knowledge use' in a way that offers another analytical understanding of knowledge transfer. He uses a typology from Broudy et al (1964) to suggest four modes of knowledge use (the examples drawn from teacher education after each are mine, not Eraut's):

1. replication (learn the formula for calculating the area of a triangle – teach pupils the formula);

2. application (learn miscue analysis for diagnosing reading difficulties – use it to diagnose a specific pupil);

3. interpretation (learn a range of behaviour management strategies – decide which is the best for this pupil);

4. association (learn about developing pupils' ability to interpret unseen poetry and recognise that this can also inform strategies for solving never-before-seen 'ill-formed' mathematical problems).

The examples above relate to transfer from codified knowledge to practice. However, the same modes of knowledge use can apply to uncodified cultural knowledge. Is the situation of use identical to the situation of acquisition so that we can replicate a performance? Do we have to interpret the situation and how we adapt our performance? Or is our mode of using earlier experience one of seeing an analogy between situations?

Eraut suggests that successful interpretation depends on 'a wealth of professional experience' (1985, p 125) so it bears a similarity to his argument that experience leads practitioners to be able to make decisions and plan actions quickly on the basis of better 'situational understanding' derived from experience. On the issue of the nature of progression from novice to expert, Eraut (2007) also draws on Dreyfus and Dreyfus's (1986) five-level model of progression. Levels 4 and 5 are shown in Table 4.2.

Table 4.2 Extract from summary of Dreyfus' model of progression (adapted from Eraut, 2007).

Level 4: proficient
Sees situations holistically rather than in terms of aspects
Sees what is most important in a situation
Perceives deviations from the normal pattern
Decision-making less laboured
Uses maxims for guidance whose meaning varies according to the situation
Level 5: expert
No longer relies on rules, guidelines or maxims
Intuitive grasp of situations based on deep tacit understanding
Analytic approaches used only in novel situations, when problems occur or when justifying conclusions
Vision of what is possible

So, if we draw on these different sources, progress in professional knowledge can be seen as developing greater ability for situational recognition, greater ability to act intuitively and greater ability to integrate different forms of knowledge in ways that make them ready to use. This leads us on to the next question.

How is professional knowledge developed?

Answering this question also requires us to think about the nature of transfer of knowledge: transfer from one form to another (eg codified knowledge to 'ready-to-use' knowledge); transfer of experience from one situation to another; transfer from one practitioner to another.

A key point about using codified knowledge in professional settings is that the amount of work needed to reconstruct it for use is underestimated. This means that much of it lies dormant and is considered irrelevant. This reconstruction is a major act of professional learning itself and someone needs to take responsibility for facilitating it. This is probably best done in the practice context by someone who understands the codified knowledge and how it can be used.

Learning to transfer what is learned from experience in one situation to another is largely a challenge of 'situational understanding' (Eraut, 2010, p 4). The only way to develop this effectively is through sustained experience. However, the nature and context of this experience is important in maximising its usefulness. This is considered below.

The main challenge for transferring learning from one practitioner to another is that much of what is important is tacit knowledge. Eraut considers other researchers' efforts to transfer tacit knowledge into codified knowledge for learning purposes and rejects them as overly optimistic (Eraut, 2004a). The key challenge is to find ways of making as much tacit knowledge as possible accessible to novices. Again the nature and context of experience helps and this is considered next.

Eraut (2007) divides professional learning opportunities into processes where learning is the main focus and processes where learning is a by-product. He also identifies a range of shorter activities that take place in either of these processes that facilitate that learning (Table 4.3).

Table 4.3: A typology of early career learning (from Eraut, 2007).

Work processes with learning as a by-product	Learning activities located within work or learning processes	Learning processes at or near workplace
Participation in group processes	Asking questions	Being supervised
Working alongside others	Getting information	Being coached
Consultations	Locating resource people	Being mentored
Tackling challenging tasks and roles	Listening and observing	Shadowing
Problem solving	Reflecting	Visiting other sites
Trying things out	Learning from mistakes	Conferences
Consolidating extending and refining skills	Giving and receiving feedback	Short courses
Working with clients	Using mediating artifacts	Working for a qualification
		Independent study

The effectiveness of these processes depends on what Eraut calls learning factors and context factors (Figure 4.1, see overleaf).

In Figure 4.1, each element within a triangle has a reciprocal relationship, and the elements that appear at the same corner on the two triangles are related. So, for example, in the top triangle, a learner's level of confidence and commitment is related to the level of challenge and the nature of trust and support. Similarly, how well we are supported (top triangle) is a result of the types of encounters and relationships we have with others (bottom triangle).

The single most important factor in effective professional learning, argues Eraut, is confidence, that results in commitment, personal agency and motivation (Eraut, 2007). However, these are not just personal qualities, they emerge relationally from the other factors in the top triangle and from the context factors in the bottom triangle. If we are given tasks with an appropriate level of challenge that we believe are important, and if we are properly supported in trusting relationships, we develop confidence and commitment. Being

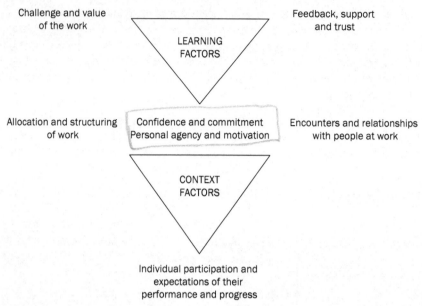

Figure 4.1 Factors affecting learning at work: the two triangle model (from Eraut 2007).

given an appropriate level of challenge depends on how carefully work is structured and allocated so that it matches our growing competence and confidence. Level and quality of support depends on how often we work with other people, rather than alone, and the type of relationship we have with them. Too much challenge, or too little support too soon, and confidence and commitment declines. Equally, too little challenge and support that might be perceived as control and we have the same problem.

In general terms, professional learning is facilitated by the opportunities that we get to work alongside others, to see others work and to talk about our work and theirs. This enables two things that are important for professional learning but that are either difficult to achieve or not achieved sufficiently. One of these is access to tacit professional knowledge and the other is frequent feedback. The more we work collaboratively the more chance we get to see others' professional knowledge in action and to talk about it. Similarly, the more chance we get for feedback on our own developing knowledge and performance. The quality of that working together and those conversations will depend on the nature of our working relationship, how much mutual trust and respect there is and how valued the novice is.

Collaborative working and high quality mutually supportive dialogue between novices and more experienced practitioners are best achieved where there is an established culture of collaborative working, mutual support and professional learning among all staff. In fact Eraut argues that a strong collaborative learning culture for experienced practitioners is the most effective contribution to learning for novices. A detailed list of factors that help and hinder workplace learning (too long to reproduce here) can be found in Eraut and Hirsh (2007).

What are the implications for ITE?

Many of the implications for ITE of Eraut's research on professional learning can be inferred from the previous section. However, it is worth considering some specific issues for current typical ITE practice.

The first relates to the frequency and richness of collaborative working between experienced teachers and student teachers. This needs to be much more sustained and to cover more aspects of the planning, teaching and assessment process than is often the case currently. This allows greater access to teachers' professional knowledge and also allows more frequent opportunities for dialogue and feedback close to practice. Linked to this is the status of the student teacher and experienced teacher as co-workers and co-enquirers rather than instructor and instructee. However, this needs to be balanced with proper respect for the student teacher's status as a novice who is there to learn not just to perform.

Eraut argues that the best context for early professional learning is one where experienced practitioners are still regularly engaged in a culture of learning and collaboration. Given that many commentators have remarked that historically teaching is a solitary profession with a weak culture of collaboration and a weak shared professional knowledge base (eg City et al, 2009), this could require a larger change of culture in the school.

A major, and overlooked, part of professional learning is learning how to transfer and integrate knowledge from different sources. Someone, regularly located in the school, needs to take responsibility for facilitating this work. It needs to be someone close to the practice of the school who also understands the codified knowledge that students will have learned. This suggests either a change in working across the boundaries of institutions or the necessity of teachers in schools using a different knowledge base.

An appropriate level of challenge can be provided by the ways that progress in the work required of novices is structured. This means thinking carefully about the sequence of tasks that are generally given to student teachers and the rationale for that sequence but also thinking about how this needs to be adapted to the progress of individual student teachers. Eraut (2000b, 2007) provides a typology of learning trajectories and a model of progression that could be a useful starting point for thinking about the rationale for the sequence although it is likely that a teacher specific model derived from this will be most useful.

On taught codified knowledge, Eraut (2012, p 41) comments that 'just in time' learning is often best. That is, learned at the point at which it becomes relevant to developing practice. This suggests a reorganisation of the relationship between academic and professional components.

It has been argued that ITE has not drawn sufficiently on research into workplace learning (McNamara, Murray and Jones 2014). McNamara, Murray and Jones seek to address that deficiency. In their concluding chapter they explore a list of factors to improve workplace learning in teacher education:

» re-focusing the status of teachers as learners;

» the importance of the adult educator in workplace learning;

» re-conceptualising support roles in teachers' workplace learning;

» (re)generating the diversity of spaces for workplace learning.

They argue that the status of both student teachers and experienced teachers as learners has been eroded as a result of cultures of performativity and newer models of teacher education. This status needs to be reclaimed for both and the complexity of that learning process acknowledged so that a culture of collective learning in schools can be (re) established.

It needs to be recognised that being a good teacher of children does not necessarily mean that teachers in school have a good understanding of how adult professional learning is best supported. Again, the complexity of that process and the specialised nature of understanding it both need to be acknowledged and thus appropriately knowledgeable people need to be involved in the process of teacher education.

This relates to the third bullet point. The current common situation in which most mentors are teachers, only minimally trained in their role, which they have to fit in alongside the day job, needs to be revisited. The status of mentoring in schools needs to be improved as does the recognition of the different set of specialist skills that it involves.

Finally, it needs to be recognised that spaces for professional practice can be created outside the school placement. Simulations, alternative placements and technology can all be used to replicate practice and foster the development of professional knowledge in authentic contexts outside of schools.

IN A **NUTSHELL**

Research into professional knowledge and workplace learning argues that professional competence is based on an integration of codified and uncodified (tacit) knowledge. It is important not to overlook the work that is necessary for the integration of this knowledge or to overlook that it needs to be facilitated for novices, not just left to happen – or not happen. Workplaces in which working and learning are seen as integrated and in which a culture of collaborative practice and ongoing learning are established are most effective at supporting the learning of novices.

REFLECTIONS ON **CRITICAL ISSUES**

Professional knowledge is an integration of uncodified and tacit knowledge and 'ready to use' codified knowledge. It is best developed through frequent collaboration and dialogue in professional contexts in a collaborative and supportive culture.

The most significant contribution of Eraut is to have analysed workplace learning through detailed long term empirical study of actual workers/learners in actual contexts to identify important processes and the factors that affect them.

Further reading

Eraut, M and Hirsh, W (2007) *The Significance of Workplace Learning for Individual's, Groups and Organisations*. SKOPE Monograph 9, Pembroke College, Oxford.

McNamara O, Murray, J and Jones, M (eds) (2014) *Workplace Learning in Teacher Education: International Policy and Practice*. London: Springer.

CRITICAL **ISSUES**

- *How coherent is the idea of communities of practice?*
- *How relevant is it to teacher education?*
- *Can it be used to enhance learning in teacher education?*

Introduction

Communities of practice has been called a paradigm shift and it is one of the most influential concepts in the social sciences in recent years (Hughes, Jewson and Unwin, 2007). Its application has spread through many professions (Hughes, Jewson and Unwin, 2007; Li et al, 2009). We could ask whether this popularity is in spite of, or because of, uncertainties about the idea of communities of practice and how it can be applied to foster professional learning. Its uses in teacher education show that it means different things to different authors and is used in different ways, not all of them consistent with one another or with the initial idea (Lave and Wenger, 1991). Inconsistencies in ideas and use can also be found between the key texts on communities of practice (Lave and Wenger, 1991; Wenger, 1998; Wenger, McDermott and Snyder, 2002). Hodkinson and Hodkinson (2004a) and Fuller et al (2005) argue that Lave and Wenger's ideas about communities of practice and their use of the ideas have diverged since they collaborated on *Situated Learning* (Lave and Wenger, 1991).

Lave and Wenger acknowledge that their early formulation of the idea was not fully developed, so this inconsistency could be a matter of evolution and development. However, we could also see it as a contradiction that calls into question the coherence of the idea (Li et al, 2009). Eraut (2002) asks whether the idea of communities of practice actually adds any explanatory value to understanding the processes of professional learning.

Communities of practice in outline

Two ideas have proved popular from the first formulation of communities of practice (Lave and Wenger, 1991): the idea of the community of practice itself and legitimate peripheral participation. The insight of communities of practice is that learning should be conceptualised as being able to participate in practices rather than acquiring knowledge 'in the head'. This participation only makes sense within a particular community of practice as a community is 'the social configuration in which our enterprises are defined as worth pursuing and our participation is recognisable as competence' (Wenger, 1998, p 5). This means that communities of practice is a theory that regards learning as situated, tied to a particular sociocultural context and set of practices. It also means that learning is about developing identity, relationships, practices and tacit knowledge as well as explicit knowledge. Learning is as much about becoming someone as learning content.

Legitimate peripheral participation is the process of learning in a community of practice. Newcomers begin with subordinate tasks and activities in the practice of the community before progressively moving into the centre of practice as they acquire more experience. Lave and Wenger report a number of specific trajectories of participation in particular communities and others have tried to identify similar trajectories in other communities of practice (Gherardi, Nicolini and Odella, 1998; Philpott, 2006).

In later formulations of communities of practice (Wenger, 1998; Wenger and Snyder, 2000; Wenger, McDermott and Snyder, 2002) the emphasis shifts from considering the development of individual learners in communities of practice to considering how communities of practice can contribute to the development of the larger organisations of which they are a part, such as companies. This involves a change from considering how newcomers appropriate existing practices and identities to considering how the community of practice working together develops new practices. To consider this, Wenger uses the idea of tensions between dualities in the system of the community of practice in a way that owes some debt to Cultural Historical Activity Theory (see Chapter 6). The resolution of these tensions develops practice. There is also a shift in emphasis from describing existing communities of practice and their associated learner trajectories to considering how communities of practice can be cultivated, often from outside by, for example, managers.

How coherent is the theory of communities of practice?

There are a number of general questions that can be asked about the coherence of communities of practice.

1. Is it empirically based or 'theoretically driven' with 'somewhat ideological overtones' (Eraut, 2002, p 12)? Eraut (2002, p 5) claims that the examples in Lave and Wenger (1991) are 'cherry picked' to support the idea. Hughes (2007) suggests that the cases in Lave and Wenger (1991) are used as illustrative examples rather than evidence. Hughes also argues that some acknowledged features of communities of practice, such as power relationships, are not evident or discussed in the examples. Lave and Wenger admit the idea of communities of practice is as much intuitive as it is derived from evidence (Lave and Wenger, 1991, p 42).

2. Is it descriptive or normative? Is community a neutral term to describe a group of people interacting or is community seen as desirable form of organisation? Community and participation seem to become normative in the teacher

education literature that espouses communities of practice. Normativity is seen in two ways: the idea of community is seen as positive rather than descriptive and what counts as a community is defined in normative ways that might differ from actual communities. 'Proper' communities are believed to be egalitarian, tolerant, welcoming of new members and open to change (Barab, Barnett and Squire, 2002; Daniel, Auhl and Hastings, 2013). Existing communities might be none of these and may only be recognisable as communities by their monocultural, conservative and closed nature (Li et al, 2009). They may also be sites of conflict or injustice. In this literature there is an elision between everyday normative uses of 'community' as in 'a sense of community' (Barab, Barnett and Squire, 2002: 525) and its use as a neutral description for interacting groups who could be dysfunctional. This normativity can also be found in Lave and Wenger where community is defined positively and communities of practice are seen as preferable ways of learning to other forms of organisation (Hughes, 2007).

3. It can be difficult to know what counts as a community of practice (Hodkinson and Hodkinson, 2004a). Li et al (2009) argue that the 14 indicators Wenger (1998) offers are too abstract. In the context of business, 'A community of practice can exist entirely within a business unit or stretch across divisional boundaries. A community can even thrive with members from different companies ... A community can be made up of tens or even hundreds of people' (Wenger and Snyder, 2000, p 141). Is this definition usefully adaptable or unhelpfully vague?

4. How do different levels of community interact in shaping practices? (Hodkinson and Hodkinson, 2004a; 2004b). Eraut (2002) argues that membership of a profession is important for professional identity but this is much larger and more diverse than a community of practice. Hodkinson and Hodkinson (2004a) suggest a change of terminology to distinguish communities of practice as small tight-knit co-located groups from wider groups that also constitute the context of practice.

Can we use communities of practice to foster learning?

Can we translate a theory that developed as an explanation of how professional learning happens into a recipe for creating professional learning (Hughes, 2007)? We can give a detailed empirically grounded explanation of how rainclouds form and why they release rain where and when they do. However, we cannot use this to form rainclouds and release rain when and where we need it because too many complex factors are outside our control even though we understand them. In Situated Learning (Lave and Wenger, 1991), it seems clear that communities of practice cannot be created at will and the theory is not intended to be one that can be applied to designing learning. However, in Wenger, McDermott and Snyder (2002), the main focus is on how to cultivate or 'nurture' (Wenger and Snyder, 2000) communities of practice. This tension can perhaps be resolved by considering a different analogy. Historically the best conditions for growing crops will have been a mystery or misunderstood. Once empirical research described the factors that promoted successful growth it became possible to ensure that the best conditions were in place to support a process that could not be forced but could be aided (Wenger and Snyder, 2000). Although we may question whether we can create communities of practice we can try to provide the best conditions for them or avoid the worst ones.

However, some issues need to be considered when using communities of practice to foster learning.

1. Membership of communities of practice is voluntary. We cannot create communities of practice and require people to participate in them. We can perhaps only create the best circumstances for communities to develop on their own and the best circumstances for existing communities to foster learning.

2. Communities of practice need a shared history (Wenger, 1998) including 'intergenerational encounters' (Wenger, 1998, p 238). This distinguishes them from other groups who work or learn together (Wenger, 1998). Community history can be in artefacts and practices as well as people. If we try to create communities, where does that shared history come from?

3. Who are the experts in purposely created communities of practice? In some of the literature on creating communities of practice in teacher education what is described looks like social constructivism rather than a community of practice (eg Barab, Barnett and Squire, 2002; Anderson and Freebody, 2005; Sim, 2006). Students collaborate to develop understanding but which community of practice are they on the periphery of and where are the expert practitioners?

4. Adapting Brown and Duguid's (1991) distinction between canonical and non-canonical practices in workplaces we can consider canonical and non-canonical communities of practice. The former are the communities of practice we might imagine exist or should exist (eg members of a department in a school). The latter are communities of practice that exist on the ground and that we might not predict (Orr, 1996). If we are cultivating communities of practice, we need to avoid basing decisions on our view of canonical communities of practice and, therefore, overlook non-canonical communities of practice.

5. Does communities of practice take account of individual differences in learners and what and how they learn (Hodkinson and Hodkinson, 2004b; Billett, 2007)? Maynard (2001) considers internal tensions that occur for learners when the practices and identity of the community are in tension with their own identity. These tensions can result in rejection of participation rather than progressive inclusion (Hodges, 1998). For Hodges (1998) this rejection was linked to a lack of historical and cultural perspective on communities of practice. The practices of some communities may enshrine culturally or historically specific world views or biases that might be unacceptable to, or marginalise, some participants.

6. Trowler (2009) suggests that issues of power and conflict are acknowledged in passing but never properly developed. Fuller et al (2005) and Fuller (2007)

argue that these issues are acknowledged in general terms in Lave and Wenger (1991), but are not present or discussed in any of the examples. This neglect of power and conflict could result from the elision of community as normative with the practices of existing communities (Jewson, 2007).

Challenges for applying communities of practice to ITE

The last section discussed challenges for applying the ideas of communities of practice in general. This section looks at issues for teacher education.

1. Engeström (2007) criticises communities of practice for identifying the working and learning practices of culturally and historically specific occupations and then abstracting them as a general theory of working and learning. Lave acknowledges the specificity of working and learning practices and accepts that we would need to investigate each separately to understand its particularities (Lave, 1996). A related concern is that the communities of practice used by Lave and Wenger may not yield insights transferrable to complex modern working and learning (Fuller and Unwin, 2003; Fuller et al, 2005).

2. Daniel, Auhl and Hastings (2013) cite Wenger's (2006) view that teaching is not yet a community of practice as it lacks the shared repertoire and mutual engagement necessary. This argument finds support from many education researchers (eg Palincsar, 1999; City et al, 2009).

3. Using the working and learning practices from the occupations cited by Lave and Wenger (1991) as a model for teacher education can downgrade the importance of formal academic learning outside the immediate context of practice (Fuller and Unwin, 2003). For teacher education Stamps' (1997) rhetorical title, *Communities of Practice: Learning is Social. Training is Irrelevant?* might stop being a question and become a statement.

4. In teacher education where is the community in which students participate? Is it teachers in schools? Is it the teachers in a particular school? Does the community include the tutors in the university? (Fuller et al, 2005). What is included in the practice of the community? Is writing essays about education part of the practice? Similar questions can be asked about legitimate peripheral participation. Would writing an education essay in the university library count as participation? Would it be *legitimate*? Is it an activity that is actually on the periphery of the community or is it outside and part of another community?

The answer to these questions partly depends on the actual practices of the community of school teachers. If teachers are a community of practice that regularly engages with academic study of their practice and collaboration with colleagues in universities to explore practice, then the academic experiences of students in universities fall within the community of practice of teachers.

Some attempts to cultivate communities of practice in teacher education try to develop such a community of practice for teachers (eg Palincsar et al, 1998; Barab, Barnett and Squire, 2002). This returns us to the normative approach to communities where we try to cultivate ideal communities rather than trying to understand what is already happening and how to maximise the benefit of this.

5. Do we envisage a model of teacher education in which students become progressively enculturated into the existing practices of a school or do we expect teacher education to result in student teachers and new teachers who will push back the boundaries of practice (Cochran-Smith, 1991; Grossman, 1991)? As before, if teachers are already pushing back the boundaries as part of a community of practice, then enculturation need not be a problem. If, however, many communities of practice favour well-established practices and tend to resist change, then enculturation could be problematic.

6. Communities of practice do not recognise the diversity of relationships and trajectories in complex working and learning situations. The *'cherry picked'* (Eraut, 2002) examples in Lave and Wenger (1991) emphasise the relationship of novice and expert in a single form of practice and a single trajectory from novice to expert, from periphery to centre. This relationship and trajectory may not represent what happens in teacher education. Teachers often comment that they welcome the new ideas that students bring and that they learn something from them (Fuller et al, 2005). The communities of practice model also does not take account of prior experience and expertise from former roles that 'novices' bring with them.

What are the implications of communities of practice for ITE?

The insight of communities of practice is that professional learning is about learning to participate in professional communities rather than just acquiring knowledge. Learning to participate is about identity, dispositions, relationships and becoming someone. It is about tacit knowledge as well as explicit knowledge (Wenger, McDermott and Snyder, 2002). These things are best developed through participation *in situ*. The theory-practice gap in ITE suggests that facilitating participation in communities of practice is better than a technical-rational approach that imparts generalised knowledge and skills that are supposed to be applied later in specific contexts (Anderson and Freebody, 2005). However, a communities-of-practice approach does bring risks. It could lead to an overemphasis on acquiring existing practice rather than transforming practice. It can also be interpreted in application as a model about replicating behaviours rather than a theorised understanding.

It is worth remembering the doubts about whether we can create communities of practice or whether we need to focus on maximising the value of existing communities. It is perhaps best used to understand what is happening in the ITE process and to think about where adjustments might be beneficial rather than as a blueprint for building new communities.

The first requirement of a community of practice is that learners have opportunities for legitimate peripheral participation in relevant communities, and this is central to their learning. However, some things need to be thought about to make this work effectively and to reduce limitations.

1. The relationship between learning through participation in the community and 'off-the-job' learning: Chapter 3 considers the advantages of demand-side learning (Brown and Duguid, 2000) and disembedding (Billett, 1998) over a model in which abstract or general understandings are first in the sequence of learning. This needs to be thought about in learning through participation in a community of practice. Some attempts to use communities of practice as a model to inform ITE have attempted to use this approach. In Barab, Barnett and Squire's (2002) 'Community of Teachers', students' school experiences are used as the starting point for learning in the university rather than abstracted general learning coming first in the sequence. It is worth considering how the sequencing of the university-based parts of ITE relate to the situated curriculum (Gherardi, Nicolini and Odella, 1998; Philpott, 2006) of legitimate peripheral participation. Philpott (2006) argues that the logic and sequence of the taught university-based component of many ITE courses is different from the logic and sequence of the situated learning curriculum of participating in schools. This makes it difficult for students to relate one to the other in what can become two separate learning journeys.

2. What do we mean by *legitimate* participation in the teaching community? In partnership schools, is the student role and identity recognised as a legitimate part of the school community? Or are students seen as outside the community proper, passing though or belonging to the university community? Or, are they not seen as *student* teachers but just as inexperienced teachers?

Although it might seem that a communities-of-practice approach requires students to be treated as teachers from the outset, this can lead to difficulties. If student teachers are seen as outside the community or are not recognised as *students* it can lead to the delegitimisation of student activities such as academic work and reflection as part of community practice. If students are seen as outside the school community of practice they do not gain the benefits of *legitimate* peripheral participation and the sense of a trajectory towards the centre of the teaching community. If students are seen as inexperienced teachers it can lead to a lack of *legitimate* space for academic study and reflection. They have a weak institutional position as learners and lose their 'learning identities' (Fuller et al, 2005). Schools need to view the student-teacher role and identity as a legitimate form of participation in the community of practice and signal that through the ways they interact with student teachers and the arrangements they make for them. Among important features of these arrangements is reification (Fuller and Unwin, 2003); the established and tangible signs of legitimacy and importance for the student role. This can be things like school-provided student handbooks, designated work spaces, specially organised regular events and proper regard given to academic work and certification. As well as reification, these can help establish the shared history important for communities of practice that indicate that a student's journey is not one off or improvised but part of established legitimate participation in the community.

3. When student teachers are not recognised as students but treated as inexperienced teachers, the speed of trajectory they take from being peripheral participants to full participants can be a problem (Fuller et al, 2005). They take the responsibilities of a teacher too quickly and this leaves insufficient space for learning. They learn to cope rather than reflect. It can also lead to only acquiring the knowledge and skills necessary for the specific functions they are given rather than learning more widely. They become full participants in the community but narrow experts (Fuller et al, 2005). They lose their identities as (legitimate) learners too quickly and gain full participation '*at the expense of ... encounter[ing] new learning possibilities*' (Fuller et al, 2005, p 58).

4. To learn from participating in practice, practice needs to be visible. Lave and Wenger (1991) cite Hutchins (1996) and Marshall (1972) to contrast participation with varying horizons of visibility. With naval quartermasters (Hutchins, 1996), relatively inexperienced participants can observe the activity of more experienced practitioners in the community as part of ordinary practice. Therefore participating in community practices provides opportunities to develop the next level of skills and knowledge. However, for meat cutters (Marshall, 1972), inexperienced members of the community cannot see much of what more experienced practitioners do. Therefore they will not learn more advanced skills from participating in community practices. The challenge for ITE is to make as much of experienced practitioners' practice visible as possible to new participants. This can be practice that is invisible because it is mental, such as decision-making processes informing planning or responding to pupils in the moment. Or it might be invisible because it falls outside what students are thought to need to know or participate in given their current role. For example, school management meetings or multi-agency meetings. The more practice that student teachers can see, the more sense they can make of their community of practice.

5. Restrictive and expansive learning (Fuller and Unwin, 2003): In restrictive learning, learners only learn what they need for the particular role they have been given in a particular workplace. In expansive learning, learners gain a wider view of how what they do fits into a bigger picture. This is a bigger picture in terms of the wider institution of which their practice forms a part and possible longer-term trajectories for their participation. One way to develop expansive learning is to give legitimacy to academic and other forms of 'off-the-job' study as this provides a different perspective on practice. Another strategy is to give learners opportunities to 'boundary cross' between communities of practice (Fuller et al, 2005). One way this happens in ITE is between school and university. However, valuable boundary crossing can be created by allowing students to participate in other communities of practice like other schools or organisations concerned with learning and young people. Boundary crossing gives a critical distance from the

practices of any one community so that practices are understood as provisional; there are other ways of practising. Boundary crossing changes the perspective from single communities to thinking about overlapping communities and how membership of several can assist expansive learning. Boundary crossing is helped by boundary brokers and boundary objects. Boundary brokers are people who are able to support moving across the boundaries of communities and the consequent expansive learning. Boundary objects are artefacts that support that process.

IN A **NUTSHELL**

The concept of communities of practice is based on the argument that learning and working are not separate activities, with learning coming before working. The concept also highlights that learning is not just about abstracted formal knowledge. The paradigm shift of communities of practice makes us look in different places for different things when we are trying to facilitate learning.

REFLECTIONS ON **CRITICAL ISSUES**

Communities of practice is a theory with tensions and blind spots in relation to ITE. However, its insights into professional learning are a valuable starting point for many who have elaborated the theory (eg Maynard, 2001; Fuller and Unwin, 2003; Hodkinson and Hodkinson, 2004a; 2004b; Fuller et al, 2005). In a time of contested ITE models, we need to ensure that it does not become a restricted model used to justify developments driven by resources and ideology.

Further reading

Hughes, J, Jewson, N and Unwin, L (2007) *Communities of Practice: Critical Perspectives*. London: Routledge.

Lave, J and Wenger, E (1991) *Situated Learning: Legitimate Peripheral Participation*. Cambridge: Cambridge University Press.

Wenger, E (1998) *Communities of Practice: Learning, Meaning and Identity*. Cambridge: Cambridge University Press.

Wenger, E, McDermott, R A and Snyder, W (2002) *Cultivating Communities of Practice: A Guide to Managing Knowledge*. Cambridge, MA: Harvard University Press.

CRITICAL **ISSUES**

- *What is Cultural Historical Activity Theory (CHAT)?*
- *How coherent is CHAT?*
- *How might an understanding of CHAT inform teacher education?*

Introduction

CHAT is a form of cultural psychology developed from Vygotsky's work. The main proponent of CHAT in Western education is Yrjö Engeström (Engeström, 1987; Engeström, Mietinnen and Punamaki, 1999). Engeström argues for three '*generations*' of CHAT, although this has been called a '*just so story*' (Bakhurst, 2009, p 201). Engeström's version of CHAT development has been largely accepted by those who apply the theory in Western education (Bakhurst, 2009) so I will use his schema in this chapter. CHAT is also best understood by following its development.

What is CHAT?

First-generation CHAT

First-generation CHAT (Engeström and Mietinnen, 1999) is Vygotsky's claim that all human activity, including learning, is mediated by historically and culturally specific tools or artefacts. Vygotsky's claim is often represented by Figure 6.1.

If the subject is a hunter and the object is a deer, the tool in question might be a stone axe or a rifle. These tools are historically and culturally specific. How the subject carries out the activity is mediated by these tools and is, therefore, the result of the cultural and historical context.

Tools need not be physical. A tool could be a scientific theory, a belief system or an established set of practices or procedures. These, also, are manufactured in particular cultural and historical contexts to help do certain jobs. So, the subject could be a scholar and the object could be an understanding of human behaviour. This activity is mediated by the culturally and historically specific theories, beliefs and practices (tools) of the context in which it happens. How the activity is approached (eg scientific experimentation or religious

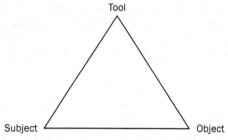

Figure 6.1 Vygotsky's tool mediation.

exegesis) and the conclusions arrived at will depend on the cultural and historical context of the subject.

First-generation CHAT has some implications for how we conceptualise learning. We should avoid understanding learning as a self-contained process inside a subject's head. Part of the structure and process of learning will come from the cultural and historical context. This means that we should not understand learning as a process that transcends culture and history. Our unit of analysis for learning needs to be the subject in a specific cultural and historical context, engaged in a specific activity so that we can study how the tools of the context mediate the learning. Tools are the products of particular cultures rather than individuals so developing their use is a form of socialisation. We therefore also need to understand learning as a social process, not an individual one.

Figure 6.1 shows two connections between the subject and the object. One, going through the apex, is the connection mediated by the tool. The second, the base, is a direct line between the subject and object. This shows that the subject has two connections to the object: one mediated and one direct. In deer hunting, the hunter has a direct physical relationship with the deer in the same way as a wolf hunting the same deer. However, the mediated connection means that they also have a historically and culturally specific connection.

This mediated connection has conceptual implications for the subject and the object. What does the deer mean and what does it mean to be a hunter within their culture and within the culturally situated activity of hunting? This mediated relationship means that the subject and object in the diagram are not identical with a flesh and blood person and deer. They represent the culturally and historically specific idea or identities of a hunter and deer participating in hunting. The identities of the subject and the object have a reciprocal (dialectical) relationship (Roth, 2004; Roth and Lee, 2007). The identity of the subject influences the identity of the object and vice versa. We cannot understand one without understanding the other. The tool enters into a dialectical relationship too. The identity of the hunter and the deer changes depending on whether the hunter kills the deer at close quarters with a stone axe or from a distance with a rifle. Changes in one part of the triadic relationship create changes in other parts, and each part can only be understood by understanding the others.

The subject, object and tool can also circulate within the relationship (Engeström, 1990; Roth and Lee, 2007). In the example of the scholar, the initial object, an understanding of human behaviour, could become a tool later on to mediate activity in relation to further objects.

Second-generation CHAT

In second-generation CHAT the triad remains but it is augmented by more detailed consideration of the features of the cultural and historical context the activity takes place in and the ways these influence the triad and one another (Figure 6.2)

Figure 6.2 emphasises that activities are collective and involve a community. An activity is not just a set of actions or something we are doing but a culturally meaningful practice that is part of what we regularly do as a culture (Roth and Lee, 2007). Hunting is an activity as is schooling or nursing.

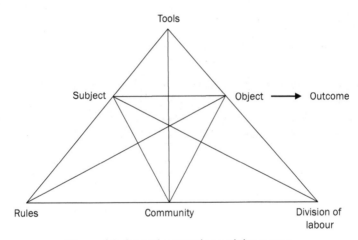

Figure 6.2 Second-generation activity system.

CHAT posits three '*levels of analysis*' (Roth and Lee, 2007) for what people do: activity, actions and operations. These are dialectically related to so that the nature of one can only be understood by understanding the nature of the others. Consider what I am currently doing as an example. At the lowest level of analysis, operations, I am pressing keys on a computer. The meaning of these operations can only be understood by locating them in the second level of analysis, the action I am engaged in – writing a book. The writing part of this is solitary. However, the meaning of this action can only be understood by locating it in the third level of analysis, the activity I am engaged in – Higher Education. As this is a dialectical relationship it also operates in the other direction. The nature of Higher Education as an activity can only be understood through an accumulation of its constituent actions, for example researching, lecturing, writing. For Higher Education to be an activity (that is something that is culturally recognised as meaningful), it must be a collective activity not something just done by one person.

The lines in Figure 6.2 indicate that the community influences the nature of the subject, the object and the tool in the first-generation triad. The dialectical nature of the activity system also means that subject, object and tools influence the nature of the community. The community itself also influences and is influenced by the other factors on the base of the triangle, rules and division of labour and in turn these influence the subject, object and tools. This representation of CHAT also includes an outcome of the activity. Second-generation CHAT expands our unit of analysis for understanding learning. We need to think about it in terms of all of the components of the specific activity system where it is taking place and the dynamic relationship between them.

Activity systems are not static systems that determine how subjects think and act within them (Roth, 2004). They are dynamic and change throughout history. The driver of this change is 'historically accumulated inner contradictions' in the system (Roth and Lee, 2007, p 203). The resolution of contradictions moves the activity system forward. Contradictions can be experienced at four levels within the system (Roth, 2004; Roth and Lee, 2007). Each below has an ITE example.

1. within any one element in the system, for example within the tools (reflective writing about lessons used as both a tool for promoting learning and as a tool for assessment and accountability; how comfortably do these purposes sit together?);

2. between two different elements in the system, for example between division of labour and object (tutors who teach students in the university and tutors (or mentors) who see students apply ideas in school are different people; does this division of labour impede the object of learning?);

3. between the activity and a culturally more advanced form of the activity (someone else is doing ITE in a way that seems to conceptualise the process more satisfactorily than we do; how long can we continue what we are doing?).

4. between a particular activity system and neighbouring one (see the next section).

Contradictions can result from the ways that the activity system has developed in the past or can come from changes outside. To understand an activity system you also have to attend to its history.

Third-generation CHAT

Figure 6.3 shows ITE represented as a third-generation activity system. The specific representations of rules, division of labour and tools are not exhaustive but indicative of the types of things that could be functioning in this way.

In third-generation CHAT the unit of analysis changes from single-activity system to the interaction between two or more activity systems. Figure 6.3 represents two different activity systems with the same object interacting.

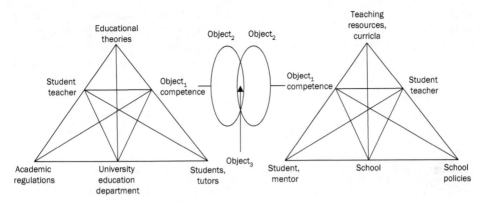

Figure 6.3 ITE as a third-generation activity system.

The object appears in three forms because the object is a conceptual construct of the activity system as well as an objectively existing phenomenon. This is represented by $object_1$ and $object_2$. $Object_2$ is an oval because the conceptual $object_2$ is uncertain and subject to change. It is emergent. If our object is student teachers' professional competence, then this is both the thing we are working on and what we are trying to achieve. How we conceptualise student teachers' professional competence within a single activity system is uncertain and subject to change.

A second activity system that also has the object of student teacher's professional competence is likely to have a different conceptualisation as it has a different community, rules, division of labour, subjects and tools. If these two activity systems interact in relation to their objects there is another possible emergent object, $object_3$, which is the area in which their two objects come into negotiation or contestation with one another.

In third-generation CHAT the unit of analysis is interacting activity systems. When we consider difficulties with learning, or enhancing the learning, of subjects we should avoid considering the subject in isolation and consider how features of the system could cause difficulties in learning or how changes to the system could enhance learning. In activity systems, historically accumulated contradictions in the system can be internalised by subjects and what are systemic difficulties can appear to be individual difficulties (Roth and Tobin, 2002).

Third-generation CHAT often focuses less on the learning of individuals and more on the ways in which activity systems, or clusters of activity systems, need to identify historically accumulated contradictions and resolve them through new forms of organisation and ways of working. If you want workers or students to improve their performance, rather than trying to develop their competence within the existing situation, you have to consider how changing the situation will result in improvements.

Engeström calls this expansive learning (Engeström, 1987). Rather than acquiring knowledge or skills that already exist and that we can learn from some authoritative source, expansive learning emphasises learning to do something new that nobody yet understands

(Engeström and Glavenau, 2012). Daniels (2004) contrasts this with the apprenticeship emphasis of some other socially based professional learning models. Engeström has developed processes for supporting clusters of activity systems to analyse their historically accumulated contradictions and to develop ways of working that resolve them (Developmental Work Research (Engeström, 1996), Change Laboratories (Engeström et al, 1996), Boundary Crossing Laboratories (Engeström, 2001)).

How coherent is CHAT?

Empirical evidence?

CHAT is a theoretically driven and derived model (Bakhurst, 2009). Although there are uses of CHAT in academic literature with empirical data, these are applications of CHAT as a framework for generating and interpreting data rather than evidence for the theory. Whereas some applications of communities of practice seek to refine the model through new empirical data (see Chapter 5) this is not often the case for CHAT.

The exponential rise in interest in CHAT (Roth and Lee, 2007) could be evidence of its validity. CHAT is used to model activity systems at a variety of levels from complete national health care systems (Engeström, 1993) to meetings involving three people (Cartaut and Bertone, 2009; Valencia et al, 2009). It can be applied in different ways to the same social organisation. For example, ITE partnerships can be analysed as single activity systems (Jahreie, 2010) or multiple activity systems (Philpott, 2006). How we identify the different elements of an activity system in a particular context can also vary.

Is this flexibility part of the value of CHAT? Or does it render it suspect (Bakhurst, 2009)? If we have wide latitude to model the same system in different ways, is there no set of circumstances that would cause us to question its validity or to feel that it needs to be revised? Does this mean that CHAT is more like an ideology rather than a theory? All empirical situations can be made to fit if we interpret them according to its presuppositions. Alternatively, Roth and Lee (2007) attribute CHAT's functioning as an *accommodating framework* (p 191) to the fact that it is a metatheory rather than a theory.

Another empirical challenge to CHAT is that it has only been used in situations that already match the activity system model (Bakhurst, 2009), situations where objects, tools and divisions of labour are already clearest and easiest to talk about. However this might bother theorists, it need not bother users of the theory. If it works where we are, perhaps we need not worry that it is not universal.

Use value possibly leads to a way out of this uncertainty about CHATs' validity. If CHAT is a heuristic (Roth and Lee, 2007) we do not need to make claims about its relationship to an existing reality. Rather we need to ask whether it yields useable results. If we use CHAT to analyse our context and this results in changes to organisation or practice that bring about the improvements in outcome we desired, then CHAT has proved its value and, in one sense, its validity.

Ideology?

Vygotsky was reconfiguring psychology to make it consistent with the ideas of Marx. Those who developed his work in the direction of activity were, in part, motivated by a desire to make it acceptable to Marxist-Leninist-Stalinist orthodoxy (Bakhurst, 2009). So does CHAT shoehorn in Marxist concepts and concerns irrespective of how well they fit learning? Some aspects of CHAT, such as division of labour, production and exchange might seem counterintuitive in a theory of learning. In addition, Engeström has retained more of the Marxist orthodoxy of activity theory than other developers of the idea (Avis, 2009).

However, a counterargument is that rethinking psychology along CHAT lines is difficult (Edwards and Daniels, 2004). It requires us to abandon many deeply held beliefs about individuals, thinking and learning. These beliefs are difficult to think outside of because they are part of folk psychology (Bruner, 1990) and because they have been part of dominant institutionalised ways of thinking for a long time. Marx argued that if the essence and appearance of things directly coincided there would be no need for science (Marx, 1894/1992). So, if CHAT sometimes argues for an essence that might feel counterintuitive, this could just be the discomfort of having to do the hard thinking that reveals that what we *think* is happening is not the same as what *is* happening.

Does CHAT commit us to particular social or political values (Martin and Peim, 2009) or is it a neutral tool for improving the functioning of individuals and systems? In Marxism, the resolution of contradictions in social organisation results in an ideologically higher form of organisation. Does the resolution of contradictions in activity systems result in a higher form of organisation or just one that is better at delivering chosen outcomes? Should we see successive resolutions in activity systems as a trajectory of cumulative progress or just as changes?

Many proponents of action research (Reason and Bradbury, 2001) see it as an approach fundamentally concerned with social justice, one that empowers marginalised voices and emancipates through challenging dominant constructions of the world. However, many practitioners use action research without that agenda. It is advocated by the beneficiaries of dominant constructions of the world (eg government departments) shorn of its ideological import (Bartlett and Burton, 2006; Cain, 2011). Should this bother us? Should we be bothered if CHAT is used in a managerialist way? (Avis, 2009).

In application CHAT often pays little attention to macro-level issues of power and conflict (Avis, 2009; Daniels, 2004). Gender, social class and ethnicity are not analysed for their effects in specific organisations or activity systems. Avis (2009) argues that CHAT in practice leads to 'transformism' rather than transformation. Rather than addressing fundamental conflicts and injustices in a way that might transform society, it resolves localised tensions and consequently sustains current dominant forms of organisation rather than challenging them. It becomes a force for conservatism (Avis, 2009). Avis (2009) also comments that, in practice, CHAT places a lot of trust in the resolution of contradictions through rational dialogue whereas these contradictions might represent entrenched privileges or power relationships that are not going to be given up or resolved easily.

Individual learner differences?

CHAT is ambivalent (Edwards and Daniels, 2004) about individual learners and the influence of individual identities on learning. Individuals in CHAT become undifferentiated ciphers in the activity system roles that they play.

How can we use CHAT in teacher education?

CHAT can be used in ITE as a heuristic to analyse current activity systems to understand how these mediate or shape current learning. A key implication of CHAT is that if we want to improve the functioning of an element in a system we need to analyse the whole system and its history to consider how it produces the results that it does. So if we are concerned that:

» students do not bring together theory and practice;

» students' reflective writing is not sufficiently reflective;

» tutor/mentor/student discussions are not as productive as we would like;

» students do not see the relevance of assignments;

» tutors do not have the sufficient research capacity;

the answer is not to address this by acting upon the individuals in question or on the processes in isolation but to consider them as an inseparable part of a whole activity system to understand how the functioning of the system as a whole and its historically accumulated contradictions shape the component parts. This means that we look for solutions by reconfiguring the system to resolve tensions.

Contemporary teacher education lends itself well to an activity theoretical analysis. Its concerns resonate with what many participants in teacher education will have experienced. It also resonates with the current organisation and recent history of teacher education. It is easy to see that there are tensions and contradictions in the system. It is easy to see these as part of the historical development of teacher education in recent decades (eg McNicholl and Blake, 2013). It is easy to see these contradictions as (in part) entering from outside the system through political intervention in both teacher education and Higher Education as a whole. It is easy to see the process as one that experiences contradictions between neighbouring activity systems (eg Snoek, 2013). These could be teacher education and pupil education. They could be Higher Education and Teacher Education. Or they could be teaching and researching (eg Potari, 2013). It is also easy to think in terms of division of labour (subject tutors, education studies tutors, visiting tutors, mentors) and tools (lesson observation forms, portfolios, teaching resources) (eg Douglas and Ellis, 2011).

Like CHAT as an analytical heuristic, developmental work research, change laboratories and boundary crossing laboratories as methods for development fit well with the organisation and practices of teacher education. Teacher education needs to work through the co-ordination of overlapping or neighbouring activity systems. Most teacher education partnerships would espouse co-operation, dialogue and partnership in spirit as important virtues. So, developmental work research, change laboratories and boundary crossing laboratories are practices that fit well with prevailing espoused values.

All of this means that it is easy to see in teacher education that enhancing professional learning might also mean enhancing the systems through which it is supposed to happen, not just changing what you do in a lecture theatre or seminar room in isolation from everything else.

The academic literature on CHAT also has examples of its use to enhance teaching and learning in schools (Roth and Tobin, 2002; Roth and Lee, 2007). CHAT argues that we should not conceptualise the learning or performance of individuals outside of the cultural and historical activity system of which they are a part. If we want to enhance the former, we need to pay attention and and redesign the latter. If we accept this as a valid position, then it applies equally to pupils learning in schools. A relatively unexplored area is whether CHAT should be taught to student teachers as a heuristic for thinking about their own teaching in schools (Kolokouri, Thedoraki and Plakitsi, 2013). There seem to be many teacher educators who apply the insights of CHAT to the learning of their own students but fewer who have extended the logic to the learning of the pupils for whom those students are responsible.

IN A **NUTSHELL**

CHAT is a theoretically driven model of cultural psychology that developed from Vygotsky's work and is informed by Marxism. CHAT emphasises that human activity, including learning, cannot be understood outside of understanding the cultural and historical context in which it happens. To improve learning we need to identify and resolve the historically accumulated tensions of the context that will be influencing learning.

REFLECTIONS ON **CRITICAL ISSUES**

The validity of CHAT could be assessed in terms of whether it works as a heuristic in practice. Does it enable us to see things we might otherwise not have seen? Does seeing those things suggest solutions we might otherwise have not arrived at? Does the implementation of these solutions produce better outcomes?

Notwithstanding doubts about the universality of CHAT (Bakhurst, 2009), the experience and organisation of current teacher education suggests that a theory that emphasises contradictions within systems and the challenges associated with multiple systems working together is a useful one for the analysis and development of learning.

In practice, for better or worse, depending on your own position, many applications of CHAT have not been noticeably ideological. It is also worth remembering that not all developments of the idea of activity in psychology have retained such apparent faithfulness to classical Marxist commitments as Engeström's. Marx's philosophical analysis of human development and its relationship to cultural and historical context might offer us valuable insights even if we do not like all the political interpretations by movements or regimes that have laid claim to Marxism (perhaps falsely).

Further reading

Douglas, A S (2014) *Student Teachers in School Practice: An Analysis of Learning Opportunities*. London: Palgrave MacMillan.

Ellis, V, Edwards, A and Smagorinsky, P (eds) (2010) *Cultural-Historical Perspectives on Teacher Education and Development: Learning Teaching*. London: Routledge.

Roth, W-M and Lee, Y-J (2007) 'Vygotsky's Neglected Legacy': Cultural-Historical Activity Theory. *Review of Educational Research*, 77(2): 186–232.

CRITICAL **ISSUES**

- *What is a clinical practice model?*
- *How does it differ from current ITE?*
- *What are the challenges for clinical practice models?*

Introduction

Support for clinical practice models of learning in ITE has recently grown among policy makers and academics (Alter and Coggshall, 2009; Grossman, 2010; NCATE, 2010; Burn and Mutton, 2013; Conroy, Hulme and Menter, 2013; McLean-Davies et al, 2013). This is the result of political challenges to the status of ITE *and* the recognition of shortcomings with current models (Ure, 2010; Zeichner, 2010). Despite this recent upturn in popularity, the advocacy of clinical practice models for ITE is not new. It can be found in the academic literature at least as far back as the 1960s (eg Hazard, Chandler and Stiles, 1967). The number of academic papers on clinical practice in ITE published in the 1970s might suggest that by the 1970s the clinical practice model was well established. So why 40 years later are recent publications sounding a '*call to action*' (NCATE, 2010) again? Why does that same literature argue that we need more empirical evidence for what works in clinical practice models (NCATE, 2010) when it would seem we should have 40 years worth.

A clue to a partial answer can be found in Warner, Houston and Cooper (1977, p 15) who by the late 1970s were already claiming a '*general lack of agreement in ITE concerning what clinical experience is, and what it is supposed to accomplish*'. In the title of their paper, it was time for *Rethinking the Clinical Concept in Teacher Education*. This alleged confusion is interesting as earlier articulations of clinical models for ITE (eg McIntosh, 1971) strongly resemble those put forward recently. In the application of the model, ITE seems to have lost its way.

Current typical ITE practices are the legacy of the developments of clinical practice in the 1970s and of later attempts to implement clinical practice models such as the Oxford internship scheme (Benton, 1990). It would seem that, in the view of recent advocates of a clinical practice model, we still have not found our way. This brief history and current state of affairs leads to two questions: how is clinical practice different from current ITE? Why, given longstanding support for the idea, have we apparently failed to implement it properly?

What is a clinical practice model?

The recent literature on clinical practice models shows a broad agreement about key features.

The primacy of school experience

Perhaps the basic claim is that school is the key site of professional learning and should therefore take priority in ITE. This can mean that school placements make up the majority of the time in ITE. It can also mean that practice in school is seen as the starting point for learning rather than as a site for applying prior learning later on. Being seen as a starting point has both a temporal aspect (placement should start early) and a conceptual aspect (learning starts with experience and moves on to theorisation rather than the reverse). If school is the key site for learning, all other aspects of ITE should be configured around the school and the needs of practice.

School experience taking priority does not mean just spending more time in school. This, in itself, has been shown to have little positive impact (Grossman, 2010; NCATE, 2010). It does not mean a reduction in the importance of educational research or theory. Clinical practice is a reassertion of their centrality to teaching and learning to teach and involves a higher profile for research activity in informing practice (Alter and Coggshall, 2009; McLean-Davies et al, 2013). ITE has been considered as a possible case of 'producer capture' (Burn and Mutton, 2013) in which the producer of a product can dictate its nature rather than the consumers or end users. However, a clinical practice model does not replace this with the idea that schools can dictate the nature of ITE ('consumer capture'?). The proposed arrangement is for genuine partnership decisions about the design and implementation of ITE and genuine partnership in its delivery, recognising that both sides bring valuable knowledge and experience.

Focusing on 'clients'

A clinical practice model should be client (pupil) focused (Alter and Coggshall, 2009; NCATE, 2010). Client focus means learning to be a teacher progresses by focusing on pupils' learning and the impact that the student teacher is having. Evaluating this impact requires careful use of data (Alter and Coggshall, 2009; Ure, 2010; Kriewaldt and Turnidge, 2013; McLean-Davies et al, 2013) and it requires reflection and conceptualisation, informed by theory and research, to understand what is happening and what needs to be done next. This focus on doing (Grossman, Hammerness and McDonald, 2009) means that all learning is intended to help answer the question what we should do next.

Developing clinical reasoning

Evaluating the current situation and planning what to do next, based on evidence and knowledge of research and theory, is referred to as clinical reasoning (Kriewaldt and

Turnidge, 2013), clinical judgment (McLean-Davies et al, 2013) or practical theorising (Hagger and McIntyre, 2006). These require the critical comparison and synthesis of different forms of knowledge such as practitioner experience and research-based theory. Clinical reasoning integrates forms of knowledge rather than privileging one over another. McLean-Davies et al (2013) also comment on the disciplinary fragmentation in university-based ITE in which psychology, sociology and linguistics might be used as frameworks in different parts of the course. Ways need to be found to explicitly consider how different forms and disciplines of knowledge can be integrated in practice rather than leaving it to chance (also see Chapter 4).

The most authentic development of clinical reasoning will occur in school. However, case studies and simulations can also be used in university (Alter and Coggshall, 2009; Grossman, Hammerness and McDonald, 2009; Grossman, 2010; NCATE, 2010). All learning in the university should help to answer the question 'what we should do next?' So rich and detailed artefacts and evidence from real classrooms should be used to think about what we need to know and what actions should be taken in specific cases. The more similar these cases are to placement schools, the better. Case studies and resources of this kind could be shared across institutions like medical or legal cases. Technology could be a resource for this (NCATE, 2010) as it can capture historical activity in classrooms and allow audiovisual access from the university to classrooms in schools.

Assessment through impact on pupils

The client focus of clinical practice means that student teachers could be assessed through evidence of their positive impact on pupils' learning. Evidence of improved pupil achievements could be the test by which student teachers would pass or fail (NCATE, 2010). Or evidence of sound clinical reasoning processes could be the criterion for passing even if positive impact on pupils cannot be demonstrated at this stage (McLean-Davies et al, 2013). This means that other assessment methods need to focus on the details of practice in the particular context of placements and should be ways of enhancing and demonstrating clinical reasoning in relation to specific pupils (McLean-Davies et al, 2013). Practitioner research is one suggested model for learning and assessment (NCATE, 2010) although Ure (2010) warns against using individual, rather than collaborative, practitioner research.

Improving the quality of school experience

School placements have a high impact on student teachers' experiences of learning to teach and the development of their abilities (Wilson, Floden and Ferris-Mundy, 2002; NCATE, 2010; Zeichner, 2010). However, they are the most variable, least quality assured and least resourced aspect of ITE (Wilson, Floden and Ferris-Mundy, 2002; Darling-Hammond, 2006; NCATE, 2010; Zeichner, 2010). Giving priority to school experience means that clinical practice models need to address these deficiencies.

There needs to be a more planned and consistent structure within the school placements (Wilson, Floden and Ferris-Mundy, 2002). This structure involves planning incremental teaching experiences that relate to a model of how teachers develop (Ure, 2010). This is not just incremental in terms of the number of hours or classes but in terms of the complexity of demands placed on clinical reasoning.

Greater proximity between chances to engage in practice and chances to consider theory that relates to that practice is needed (Arnold et al, 2012). This is primarily temporal proximity but this is assisted logistically if it is also proximity of location.

Changing roles in ITE

Proximity of location implies one of two things (or perhaps both): that university tutors are located in school for more time than is currently the case and that school-based colleagues are better equipped to join theory and research to experience.

Clinical practice models advocate changing or breaking down current role distinctions and relationships and current institutional and location boundaries. We might need to enhance the ability of mentors to teach about theory and to carry out research. University tutors might engage in more teaching of pupils in schools. This could be a realignment of roles and locations or it could be the dissolution of some existing distinctions in identity and role. Greater use of joint school/university appointments is advocated (NCATE, 2010). More rigorous training and certification of participants such as mentors is also required (Grossman, 2010; NCATE, 2010; Zeichner, 2010; Kriewald and Turnage, 2013) and more time needs to be allocated to 'school-based' colleagues to carry out their roles (NCATE, 2010)

There needs to be a change in the student teacher/mentor relationship. In clinical practice models they are co-enquirers focusing on the learning of pupils (Kriewald and Turnage, 2013). The student teacher and the mentor use clinical reasoning to plan the next steps, with the mentor modelling clinical reasoning and scaffolding the student's developing clinical reasoning. This approach can provide the visible thinking that Shulman (2005) argues is central to 'signature pedagogies' in professions. This approach requires more team teaching and less solo teaching (Grossman, 2010; Ure, 2010)

Communities of enquiry

These changes are intended to result in a professional community with an inquiring stance (Kriewald and Turnage, 2013) in which teaching, learning, researching and mentoring are shared roles and in which individual participants might change roles at different times (Grossman, 2010; NCATE, 2010; Zeichner, 2010; Kriewald and Turnage, 2013; McLean-Davies et al, 2013). Another aspect of developing this community can be placing several students in each school or department so that peer feedback and support is available (Benton, 1990; McLean-Davies et al, 2013). ITE can also be joined with the ongoing professional development of all staff so that student teachers and experienced teachers participate in the same learning opportunities (Grossman, 2010; Conroy, Hulme and Menter, 2013; McLean-Davies et al, 2013). Staff members responsible for student teacher development can also be responsible for wider professional development (not forgetting the fluidity and mutability of roles that means all teachers will be learners and teachers at different times).

An ITE to CPD continuum

Removing the distinction between ITE and ongoing professional development means some current clinical practice models place student teachers in schools that will employ them (Grossman, 2010). This is intended to enhance the authenticity and relevance of what student teachers learn and also to provide continuity in professional development. Continuity can also be provided by continuing a structured professional development relationship with student teachers beyond initial training (Alter and Coggshall, 2009; Grossman, 2010).

Frequency and quality of feedback

Frequent focused high-quality feedback on practice is necessary for effective professional learning (Grossman, 2010). Maximising the frequency, focus and quality of feedback is important. This is enabled by the increased proximity of experience and theory-informed reflection, changed locations and roles for mentors and tutors, mentor and student as co-enquirers and the availability of peer feedback. The use of simulations and role play for learning in university can also increase opportunities for feedback on practice (Grossman, 2010).

Changing the nature of schools

The clinical practice model does not rely on giving student teachers increased or enhanced access to existing practice in schools. It relies on transforming practice in schools at the same time as it transforms ITE. Some developments of clinical practice models have been connected to concerns about pupils' achievements in school as much as they have to concerns about the nature of ITE (NCATE, 2010). Joining up these concerns is intended to better prepare the next generation of teachers for the specific challenges of the schools they will work in and also transform the current practice in those schools.

The mismatch between the vision of a clinical practice model and current arrangements and practices in schools has meant that a number of existing examples of the model have used a limited number of specialist partner schools that have agreed to develop their own organisation and practices in order to accommodate the model (NCATE, 2010; Grossman, 2010).

Ending fragmentation in ITE

All of these recommendations are designed to end the 'fragmentation' (Grossman, 2010) or 'segmentation' (NCATE, 2010) in ITE that inhibits effective development of professional practice in students.

The importance of evidence

A robust evidence base is fundamental to the idea of clinical reasoning. A robust evidence base is also important throughout the clinical practice model. Many existing clinical practice models, and advocates of the model, emphasise the importance of using robust evaluation and evidence to monitor and develop the model (NCATE, 2010; McLean-Davies et al, 2013). This is both evaluating particular models and building up a centralised evidence base of what works that can be used as a resource for all developers (NCATE, 2010; Grossman, 2010). NCATE (2010) also suggest that programme approval should be based on evidence of impact on pupils' learning in partnership schools.

What are the challenges for clinical practice models?

The arguments for clinical practice models seem plausible and persuasive. They have been broadly consistent in published work since the 1960s. Some commentators refer back to Dewey's work in 1904 as a source (Grossman, Hammerness and McDonald, 2009; Zeichner, 2010). So why do academics and policy makers still need to advance the same arguments with the same urgency? Why has more progress not been made? The challenges for clinical practice models can be divided into two groups: practical and conceptual.

Practical challenges

One practical challenge is the inter-institutional and intra-institutional changes that are necessary to end 'fragmentation'. In schools, these require changes in practice, role, internal organisation and culture, with consequent resource issues. These include changes to roles, for example of mentors, who need to be given more time to do their job. They also include wider cultural changes in schools so that teaching that is seen by many as largely personal, intuitive and individualistic (Alter and Coggshall, 2009; Kriwaldt and Turnidge, 2013) becomes collaborative and evidence based. These types of changes are not under the control of universities.

Organisational and cultural changes are also required in universities. The roles and location of staff need to change. There could be particular challenges relating to staff professional identity and careers (Zeichner, 2010). ITE in universities has been accused of 'academic drift' (Grimmett, Fleming and Trotter, 2009) in which the status and career of academic staff is tied to criteria derived from more traditional areas in the university. So publications and research income generation become important for status and progression. Spending more time in schools working with pupils, teachers and student teachers may not be appealing. In practice these roles (and joint school-university appointments) are taken by colleagues on teaching contracts or secondments from schools (Zeichner, 2010). This reintroduces the fragmentation and status hierarchy between researchers, theorists and practitioners. To change this structure of status and reward requires changes at least at university level.

There are also possible regulatory and legal problems because of the obligations placed on institutions, both financially and in relation to their mission. These might be compromised by the need of a clinical practice model for more cross-institutional mission and resourcing (NCATE, 2010).

Resource issues are challenging. There is the reallocation of resources within institutions. For example, those in schools that would allow mentors more time to work with student teachers or those in universities that would fund additional mentor training. This can also entail resources moving across institutions or being shared by institutions and can require agreement beyond the university course, department or partnership school. Clinical practice models also cost more than current models (NCATE, 2010). How likely is this to be possible in a time of increasingly constrained resources? Many politically favoured models of ITE that put schools at the centre tend to be cheaper than the current model. It is a moot point whether this is part of their attraction. A number of existing clinical practice models have been paid for with additional project funding (Zeichner, 2010; Conroy, Hulme and Menter, 2013). This, and the need for substantial commitment from partner schools, raises questions about the scalability of these models (Alter and Coggshall, 2009). This may account for the limited impact that existing and historical clinical practice models have had on ITE (Burn and Mutton, 2013).

These challenges mean that the development of scalable and sustainable clinic practice models might require changes at whole institutional, regional and even national level to be achieved (Alter and Coggshall, 2009). This is why NCATE (2010) in its 'call to action' on clinical practice models includes a list of actions at state and national level as well as at institutional level.

The impact of existing models might also be low because of the relative absence of useable research evidence on the clinical practice model (Wilson, Floden and Ferrini-Mundy, 2002; Alter and Coggshall, 2009; NCATE, 2010; Burn and Mutton, 2013; Conroy, Hulme and Menter, 2013), although there is evidence relating to specific aspects of the model. The research evidence that exists shows mixed results and does not necessarily address the issues that would be important to inform the design and development of future models. This is why one of the central calls of proponents of clinical practice models is for more empirical evidence. It is envisaged that this empirical evidence would be shared collectively as part of the evidence-based practice that suffuses the clinical practice model.

Conceptual challenges

Practical challenges to developing clinical practice models do not invalidate the model itself. However, questions can be raised about the fundamental idea of the model. These questions centre on the idea of evidence-based practice.

Is the term clinical practice a value neutral description of a particular approach to ITE? Or does it carry with it the spurious allure of the certainty and progress of medical practice? Not to mention its status? Clinical practice models tend to adopt much of the discourse of medicine such as diagnosis and intervention (OECD, 2011; Kriewaldt and Turnidge, 2013;

McLean-Davies et al, 2013). Proponents of the model report, approvingly, that teachers and student teachers begin to adopt this discourse even though it seems '*uncomfortable*' at first (Kriewaldt and Turnidge, 2013; McLean-Davies et al, 2013). Are the proponents not only using the discourse but also 'captured by the discourse' (Bowe, Gewirtz and Ball, 1994) such that they strive after the certainty of evidence-based practice in medicine in a profession where this might not work? Is part of the appeal of the clinical practice model this (illusory) promise of certainty and progress in a profession that has been vilified for apparent lack of progress?

References to academic literature on medical education and clinical reasoning in medicine tend not to include any references to the problematisation or critique of these ideas in medicine itself (Roegman and Riehl, 2012). So they present an idealised model of clinical practice rather than one that engages with the specific strengths and weaknesses of actual medical education and clinical practice.

Hammersley (2005) argues that a belief in evidence-based practice in education, which can be driven by political imperatives, sets expectations too high for the relationship between research and practice. This results in a sense of failure and blame when it does not happen. He argues that there are a number of necessary mismatches between the nature and needs of educational research and practice. To try to overcome or ignore these runs the risk of distorting research or practice, or both.

Biesta (2010) critiques the idea of evidence-based education in terms of three deficits: a knowledge deficit (research evidence can only ever tell us what has happened in the past and not what will happen in the future); an efficacy deficit (social structures are '*open, recursive, semiotic*' (p 497) systems in which '*interventions do not generate effects in a mechanistic or deterministic way*' (p 497)); and an application deficit (what is developed in one place cannot be applied in another unless we make the site of application more like the site of development).

Grimmett, Fleming and Trotter (2009, p 5) counsel against '*mimetic isomorphism*' under the influence of '*macro-political neo-liberalist pressures*'. This entails one organisation (ITE) seeking legitimacy by '*aping*' another (medicine). They also warn against the risk of reducing diversity. In medicine it might make sense to strive for a single agreed best practice for treating a physical condition based on shared and directly comparable evidence. However, to reduce ITE to a single agreed best practice model, as advocacy of a central repository of what works might suggest, is risky. In their words: '*The field of genetics instructs us that the more we reduce diversity, the more we expose life to quick destruction*' (p 5).

IN A **NUTSHELL**

The difference between clinical practice models and current models of ITE might be captured by NCATE's (2010) phrase that we need to turn ITE on its head. A clinical practice model emphasises school practice as the starting point for learning and configures other aspects of ITE around this. Clinical reasoning is seen as the main goal of ITE so that all learning should be helping to answer the question what we should do now in this particular situation. The model emphasises the importance of evidence-based practice both in terms of what teachers learn about teaching and also in terms of the ways the model itself is developed. In organisational terms the model seeks to end the fragmentation of ITE by dissolving many of the boundaries that currently exist in institutions, roles and elements of ITE courses.

REFLECTIONS ON **CRITICAL ISSUES**

The model faces many organisational and resource challenges that require support or agreement from beyond ITE courses themselves. However, it is possible that some progress can be made in adopting elements of clinical practice models even without significant institutional changes (Zeichner, 2010), for example, changing patterns of placements and adopting case study and simulation methods in university sessions. Some of the increased proximity (temporal and location) of experience and informed reflection can also be achieved through technology.

The significance we attach to critiques of evidence-based practice for clinical practice models will depend on the role of evidence-based practice in our conception of clinical practice in ITE. It is an important idea to many proponents of the model. However, it is possible to retain the idea that learning starts from experience and that experience needs to be reflected on using theory and research without having to adopt a positivist evidence-based practice model. It is similarly possible to recognise that current ITE practice might be fragmented in ways that hinder symbiosis of theory, research and experience and to believe that clinical practice models might be the way forward, while recognising the problems with a simple conception of evidence-based practice.

Further reading

Burn, K and Mutton, T (2013) Review of 'Research-Informed Clinical Practice' in Initial Teacher Education, BERA. [online] Available at: http://www.bera.ac.uk/wp-content/uploads/2014/02/BERA-Paper-4-Research-informed-clinical-practice.pdf (accessed 21 July 2014).

Grimmett, P P, Fleming, R and Trotter, L (2009) Legitimacy and Identity in Teacher Education: A Micro-Political Struggle Constrained by Macro-Political Pressures. *Asia-Pacific Journal of Teacher Education*, 37(1): 5–26.

Hammersley, M (2005) The Myth of Research-Based Practice: The Critical Case of Educational Inquiry. *International Journal of Social Research Methodology*, 8(4): 317–30.

NCATE (2010) Transforming Teacher Education through Clinical Practice: A National Strategy to Prepare Effective Teachers. [online] Available at: http://www.ncate.org/LinkClick.aspx?fileticket=zzeiB1OoqPk%3D&tabid=715 (accessed 21 July 2014).

CRITICAL **ISSUES**

- *What is craft knowledge?*

- *What do we mean by apprenticeship?*

- *What would an apprenticeship model of ITE look like?*

Introduction

In ITE there is ambivalence about the idea of teaching as a craft and learning to teach as an apprenticeship. This ambivalence hinges on what we understand by 'craft' and 'apprenticeship' and the ways that these words are used differently by different people.

What is craft?

'Craft' is often defined oppositionally as less than either 'art' or 'profession'. In teaching, Shulman (1986) locates the distinction between craft and profession in the use of strategic knowledge. For Shulman, craft is an activity defined by applying known procedures to routine situations. Being a professional is defined by a less routine fit between situations and procedures. For a profession, strategic knowledge is needed to make judgments about what the appropriate response is to novel situations or situations that are never the same in every detail. The fit between the situation and the response is never straightforward. It is a kind of informed improvisation or performance.

In ITE the idea of teaching as a craft, rather than a profession, has been associated for some people with the erosion of the status of teaching. This, they argue, has resulted from a series of educational reforms including the National Curriculum, competence-based models of ITE, the increasing location of ITE in schools and downplaying of the status of its academic components. This seems to be based on a model of teachers as technicians who are expected to be trained (rather than educated) to competently 'deliver' the content, strategies and techniques that have been decided elsewhere, presumably by those more knowledgeable. It also seems to be based on the idea that the specialist knowledge of teaching is relatively low-level procedural knowledge easily acquired on the job.

However, although 'craft' can often be defined negatively as falling short of 'art' or 'profession', 'craftsman' and 'craftsmanship' are terms that are generally viewed positively. They conjure up images of someone who is in total command of their work. Sennett

(2008) writes of the craftsman as someone concerned with achieving perfection for its own sake, who is motivated by love of the work (in this chapter references to craftsman or, later, masters should be considered gender neutral). Sennett also argues that '*making is thinking*' in craftsmanship (Sennett 2008, p ix). He rejects the dichotomy of thinking first and doing afterwards and its associated implication that thinking is superior. Other writers on craft knowledge (Gamble, 2001; Grimmett and MacKinnon, 1992) make a similar point that thinking and doing are not separated as a duality in which we think first and then do. Doing and thinking are inseparably blended so that doing is thinking.

Similarly, studies of craftsmen who work with physical materials emphasise craftsmanship as an evolving skilled performance in response to the developing state of the work (Keller and Keller, 1996; Wood, 2004). In Keller and Keller's study of blacksmithing and Wood's study of wood turners, both emphasise the ways in which craftsmen subtly adjust what they are doing in an ongoing response to complex cues (sight, sound, feel) in an ever-changing situation. Likewise, Gamble (2001), discussing apprentice cabinetmakers, writes about the '*workmanship of uncertainty*' and '*free workmanship*' where '*the end-result depends on the judgment, care and dexterity of the worker*' (p 182).

These writers on craft do not view it as the simple application of a fixed procedure to routine situations. They view craft as a skilled performance in response to situations that are unknown and changing. So appropriating the term 'craft' as a negative comparison to something considered superior may be more common among those who do not have detailed experience of what craft is. This richer conception of craft can also be found in the literature on teachers' craft knowledge (Rigano and Ritchie, 1999; Leinhardt, 1990; Grimmett and MacKinnon, 1992).

Ambivalence about the term craft can be found in ITE. On the one hand there are those who use it as an unfavourable comparison with their preferred conception of teaching as profession (Jarvis, 2005). On the other there are those who see the identification of teachers' craft knowledge as a way to strengthen the status of teachers as people who possess complex specialist knowledge not possessed by others (Leinhardt, 1990; Burney, 2004; Black-Hawkins and Florian, 2012). The idea of teachers' craft knowledge has been used in this way to bolster the status of teaching as a profession, to argue for the unique specialist knowledge base of teacher education, and to bolster the status of teachers in relation to other groups in education such as education researchers or governments. This enterprise finds an echo in Gamble (2001) who contrasts the expertise, control and autonomy of the craftsman over the whole process and product of work with the erosion of power and status that results from a Taylorist approach to manufacturing that breaks production down into a sequence of unskilled steps. So whereas for teaching the idea of craft is seen by some as a diminution of status and autonomy, in manufacturing craft is seen as the guarantee of status and autonomy.

What is apprenticeship?

Apprenticeship is a similarly contested and uncertain term. Aldrich (1999) questions whether it is '*a catch all term to describe a variety of practices which have been, and remain, essentially different'* (p 14). This uncertainty may be compounded by increased co-opting of the term apprenticeship for theories of learning outside of apprenticeship as a set of institutional arrangements for workplace learning. Apprenticeship as an actual form of workplace organisation and apprenticeship as a theory of (or prescription for) learning may not be the same thing.

Where apprenticeship has negative connotations it can be characterised as 'sitting with Nellie'. In this conception, new workers learn to replicate existing routine practices while participating on the job in a way not distinguished from that of other workers. However this image is probably more typical of unskilled or semi-skilled work and can be quite different from the actual practice of apprenticeship in skilled work. Paradoxically, as the revival of interest in apprenticeships in industry emphasises the importance of academic study and certification away from the workplace (Evans et al, 2006), apprenticeship as a model for teacher education is often seen, by its critics, as marginalising the importance of the same things.

Like 'craft' there is ambivalence towards the idea of apprenticeship in ITE. On the one hand it can be used pejoratively for forms of ITE that critics believe overemphasise the replication of school-based behaviours over academic study and conceptual understanding. On the other hand it has been enthusiastically embraced in the form of communities of practice (Lave and Wenger, 1991) and cognitive apprenticeship (Rogoff, 1990) as a richer and more illuminating model of learning than those that preceded it.

Cognitive apprenticeship focuses on close collaboration as a means of developing complex processes of thinking rather than replicating fixed actions. Whether we view apprenticeship as an impoverished or rich model of learning will depend on what we think is to be learned through the apprenticeship. Grimmett and MacKinnon (1992) argue that what we consider to be the craft knowledge of teachers will depend on how we conceptualise the role of the teacher: transmitter of knowledge or facilitator of autonomous enquiry. Similarly, how we view the adequacy of apprenticeship will depend on how we conceptualise craft knowledge: the replication of routine procedures or skilled and responsive performance in a context of change and uncertainty.

There are overlaps between the ideas in this chapter and those in other chapters. Van Driel, Verloop and de Vos (1998) locate research into Pedagogical Content Knowledge (Chapter 3) as part of the larger project of research into teachers' craft knowledge. Ideas of apprenticeship play an important part in communities of practice (Chapter 5). There are also similar emphases in Eraut's research into workplace learning (Chapter 4) and in clinical practice models (Chapter 7). This suggests that the underlying ideas in this chapter find favour in teacher education despite the concern they provoke in some of their manifestations. Consequently, this chapter will mainly focus on providing a counterweight to concerns resulting from deficit models of craft and apprenticeship by asking how our understanding of teaching and learning to teach can be enhanced rather than diminished by adopting the idea of teaching as a craft, and learning to teach as apprenticeship. It will also ask what an adequate apprenticeship model for teacher education would look like compared to the impoverished models that critics (and some proponents) might imagine.

How does viewing teaching as a craft enhance our understanding?

Focussing on the nature of teachers' craft knowledge recognises the specialist knowledge and expertise of teachers as something distinct from other groups, such as graduates in the same subject(s), education researchers, education academics and government education departments. This specialism and expertise underpins the status of teachers as a distinct profession with unique insight into the process and practice of schooling. Rather than undermining teachers' status, recognition of this craft knowledge is what bolsters it. A related benefit is that focussing on understanding and developing craft knowledge can be the unique contribution of teacher educators (including teachers) that underpins their identity and status in higher education in relation to other types of academics (MacNamara and Desforges, 1978).

The idea of craft knowledge emphasises the importance of performance in learning to teach. Rather than a primary focus on acquiring bodies of knowledge or collections of generic techniques, beginning teachers have to learn to act in response to novel and changing situations. Focusing on craft knowledge puts a primary focus on developing the ability to recognise situations, respond in the moment and monitor and adjust actions as necessary. This type of performance includes reflection-in-action (Schön, 1990) and the ability to recognise situations and respond in increasingly intuitive ways (Eraut and Hirsh, 2007).

The focus on craft as performance requires that we recognise that knowledge in use is integrated. The nature and process of this integration should be part of what we study and seek to develop (see also Chapters 4 and 7). Traditional approaches to teacher education separate out different forms of knowledge. Codified knowledge relating to psychology or to a school subject might be acquired in a lecture. Experiential knowledge relating to the behaviour of pupils might be acquired during a placement. In use these different forms of knowledge have to be integrated. If we do not recognise the importance of the craft knowledge of performance, there is a risk that we leave this integration to chance and an associated risk that some of this knowledge (typically the codified knowledge) comes to be seen as irrelevant because it is not clear how it can be used in the specific situations of practice.

The integration of knowledge in doing also draws our attention to the importance of forms of knowledge that cannot easily be articulated or communicated outside of doing. This includes tacit knowledge. It can also include learning that relates to physical aspects of being and acting in a specific context. Wood (2004) writes about an experienced wood turner responding to the sound and feel of the turning wood to decide to change tools during the turning process. When questioned he initially struggled to identify what had prompted the decision and what made the new tool more appropriate. His decision was based on past and present physical experience. Zuboff (1988) writes about technicians in a paper mill who found it difficult to manage the production process when they were relocated to a new control room off the shop floor. The control room was supplied with fine-grained, accurate and frequently updated data about production. However, the technicians had not recognised until that point how much of their understanding of the process and whether to intervene was based on cues such as sound and vibration. Similarly, both Wood (2004) and Gamble (2001) write about craftsmen physically adjusting the hand positions of novices rather than communicating feedback verbally.

These are examples from physical crafts and industry. However we can think of aspects of listening to the 'back talk' (Schön, 1990) of classrooms that rely on similar sensory cues often below the threshold of conscious reflection. We can also think of times when feedback to beginning teachers is best achieved by physically modelling rather than verbally describing. Thinking of teaching knowledge as craft knowledge ensures that we do not neglect the importance of these aspects of learning and performing by over emphasising codified knowledge and knowledge that can be acquired and communicated verbally. It also ensures that we do not neglect the centrality of doing in authentic contexts to develop this aspect of the craft of teaching.

The integrated nature of knowledge in use and the importance of non-codified forms of knowledge also relates to personal and interpersonal aspects of teaching such as values and relationships. Aldrich (1999) writes of historical apprenticeships that, unlike more recent forms of education, they did not separate skills and knowledge from values and relationships. These were integrated in the process of learning. Tom (1980) writes of teaching as a 'moral craft' that should not separate values from technique. A craft conception of teacher knowledge, rather than reducing it to low-level technical procedures, can integrate values with practice in ways that a research-based 'applied science metaphor' (Tom, 1980, p 322) might not.

Focussing on the craft of performance as central to learning to teach also suggests that we have to reconfigure the relationship between codified knowledge and performance. Learning codified knowledge has to follow the needs of doing. This could mean that it is introduced when it is necessary to improve performance rather than ahead of performance. Or it could mean that codified knowledge needs to be learned in the context of use so that it is more easily related to the uses it is put to. The context of use can either mean learning in the physical location of practice or it can mean that learning disciplinary knowledge, for example, could start from considering how pupils typically understand a particular topic (also see Chapter 3).

A craft understanding of teachers' knowledge puts the main emphasis on student teachers learning effectively to *do* teaching – not learning to write essays about teaching or have discussions about teaching. Every aspect of teacher education content and 'delivery' then has to be evaluated for how successfully it contributes to this central outcome.

What does an understanding of apprenticeship offer to our understanding of teacher education?

The defining feature of apprenticeship is early and sustained participation in practice under the close guidance of a master practitioner. Critics of apprenticeship as a model for ITE are often concerned that it focuses on replicating existing behaviours rather than conceptual understanding, reflection or innovation. However, some proponents of apprenticeship approaches have argued that early learners need models that they can emulate before they have the confidence to move on to criticality and innovation (McNamara and Desforge, 1978; Maynard and Furlong, 1995). Criticality and innovation come from a position of security with current practice, they argue, rather than from novices who might be struggling with the basics.

The criticism that apprenticeship models lead to replication of existing behaviours is only a criticism if we assume that the behaviours being replicated are unreflective and lacking in innovation. Where we view craft as a skilled performance adapting to changing circumstances, the behaviour that novices will learn to replicate will itself be reflective and adaptive. This is apprenticeship comparable to cognitive apprenticeship rather than 'sitting with Nellie'. If it is skilled performance we want novices to learn, then apprenticeship with currently skilled performers can be a more effective way of doing this than academic study remote from the context of practice. Similarly, learning a skilled performance in this way means that different forms of craft knowledge, including values and relationships, are integrated in what is learned rather than this integration being left to chance at a later time. The integration of different forms of knowledge includes tacit knowledge. If we accept that tacit knowledge is an important part of what skilled practitioners develop and draw on in the practice, we must accept that this form of knowledge is best learned through sustained participation in practice.

Gamble (2001) comments that the visibility of the whole cabinet-making process to apprentices in the workshop means that they can relate any part of the process they are learning to the whole and, therefore, have a better understanding of it. Apprenticeship models of ITE presume a sustained period spent in school, from early in the process, participating in all aspects of school life. This means that aspects of practice that novices learn will be in the context of their understanding of the whole of schooling. This is preferable to a situation in which discrete aspects might be learned in a context away from the totality of practice (ie the HEI) before experience of practice as a whole has been developed. This will make it more difficult for novices to understand the part they are learning about in relation to the whole and they will, therefore, have a lesser understanding of the part.

Beginning the learning process with sustained participation in practice means that codified or other forms of knowledge that are learned are learned in the context of need and application. This is likely to lead both to a better understanding of what is relevant about this knowledge and more chance that it will be applied in practice.

What would an adequate apprenticeship model for ITE look like?

Concerns about adopting apprenticeship models in ITE might be based on concern that the current limitations of ITE school placements would be extended across the whole process of learning. However, an adequate apprenticeship model would require a significant reorganisation of practice in schools and of ITE in schools. It would not just mean reducing the amount of HEI time and input. This might be as much of a surprise to some current proponents of apprenticeship-based models as to critics.

Apprenticeship requires close collaboration with a skilled practitioner over a sustained period. It typically takes craft apprentices 5 to 7 years to attain mastery or journeyman status. Why should teaching take less time? This requirement for close collaboration and time means that apprentices in ITE would need to work more closely, for longer and on more aspects of teaching with skilled practitioners than is typically the case in ITE placements. Currently it is not unusual for novices to be left alone quite early on and for there to be very little sustained collaboration around, for example, planning and assessing. Guidance from 'masters' typically comes relatively infrequently and in limited forms, perhaps once a week, through a limited model of observation and verbal feedback on classroom performance. The time requirement means that the current one-year model for postgraduate ITE would need to be extended with a longer period of apprenticeship. Perhaps beyond the initial period of apprenticeship, novices could become journeymen, still recognised as learners rather than practitioners who are expected to take on the full workload of masters.

Apprentice cabinet makers are not expected to learn by making complete cabinets. They are given subsidiary tasks appropriate to their level of development until they are ready to complete the full task. Much of student teachers' learning is expected to proceed by giving them full responsibility for the entire teaching, learning and assessment process early on. An adequate apprenticeship model for ITE would recognise that more time needs to be spent working on appropriate subsidiary tasks in a situated curriculum (Gherardi, Nicolini and Odella, 1998) with an appropriate 'horizon of observation' (Hutchins, 1996) that would allow them to learn about and move on to the next stages.

An adequate apprenticeship model would also need to give more consideration to how skilled practitioners' tacit knowledge can be accessed by novices. Sustained close collaboration helps, but novices would also benefit from being trained in identifying what requires explanation in skilled practice and how to elicit this (Rigano and Ritchie, 1999). Conversely, skilled practitioners need to be developed in terms of their ability to recognise and articulate the nature of their tacit knowledge. There is perhaps a role for teacher educators who could study how to elicit, capture and communicate tacit knowledge most effectively (see Wood, 2004, 2006, for the educational expertise required for doing this).

In Japan, the dominant conception of teacher knowledge is craft knowledge (Shimahara, 1998). Teachers' professional development (including early development) makes little use of higher education and proceeds through collaboration among teachers. However, for this to happen, the culture of schools in Japan is significantly different from that of many schools in the United Kingdom. There is an established culture of collaboration within and between schools, with frequent timetabled visits to colleagues' classrooms and schools. There is an accepted culture of regular focused peer observation and lesson study. Proper planning, time and resource has to be allocated by school management. An adequate apprenticeship model in the United Kingdom would require the development of a similar culture and the allocation of similar resources. It could not operate just by placing student teachers in the practice context of many existing schools. Despite the time allocated for these activities, Shimahara reports that they still result in a heavy workload and burnout for many teachers. An apprenticeship model that is adopted without sufficient planning, time, space and resource given to learning for all teachers runs the risk of Kelly's (2006) titular complaint about apprenticeship models of learning in medicine: '*Too busy to think, too tired to learn*'.

Recent researchers into apprenticeship models of learning in industry have identified the importance of off-the-job academic learning and certification for the quality of apprenticeship learning (Evans et al, 2006). In teacher education too, therefore, an apprenticeship model would need to avoid marginalising this form of learning and certification.

One final observation on an adequate apprenticeship model for ITE can be taken from Rikowski (1999). Rikowski observes that historically the status of being an apprentice was time limited. Once an apprentice became a master they had autonomy over the nature of their future learning, practice and the training of future apprentices. Rikowski argues that we have entered a stage of post-modern apprenticeship in which we never escape being apprentices because the terms of our work and learning are set from outside and goal posts are always shifting. Post-modern apprentices never achieve the status or autonomy of a master. Arguably, an adequate apprenticeship model for ITE would need to restore the autonomy of mastery to teachers rather than leaving it in the hands of government.

IN A **NUTSHELL**

A craft model of teacher knowledge is as likely to bolster the status of teachers as it is to diminish it. Craft knowledge can mean skilled and responsive performance as much as replicating standard procedures. Craft knowledge integrates forms of knowledge that are unhelpfully separated by some forms of ITE. An apprenticeship model of teacher education would not mean putting student teachers 'in at the deep end' in the context of current school practice, consequently marginalising the complexity of learning and what there is to be learned. It would require considerably more planning, time and resource to be given to the learning of all teachers.

REFLECTIONS ON **CRITICAL ISSUES**

Craft knowledge is the knowledge that skilled teachers have that allows them to act in complex and changing situations. It integrates several forms of knowledge including codified knowledge, tacit knowledge and values. Apprenticeship requires a sustained and close relationship with skilled practitioners collaborating on all aspects of the teaching and learning process in order to access this craft knowledge in its integrated form. It requires planning in terms of the sequence of activities that learners engage in. An apprenticeship model for ITE would require that learning from one another through collaboration, reflection and discussion was a more planned, better resourced and more central aspect of the practice of all teachers and that novice teachers were not left to work alone too early with only occasional observation and feedback.

Further reading

Grimmett, P P and MacKinnon, A M (1992) Craft Knowledge and the Education of Teachers. *Review of Research in Education*, 18: 385–456.

Hagger, H and McIntyre, D (2006) *Learning Teaching from Teachers; Realizing the Potential of School-Based Teacher Education*. Maidenhead: Open University Press.

CHAPTER 9 | **CONCLUSION**

CRITICAL **ISSUES**

- *What can the theories of professional learning in this book, taken collectively, teach us?*

Introduction

The introduction to this book sets out some of the differences in focus and emphasis that can be found in theories of professional learning.

This chapter will consider what the theories in this book have in common. The value of this is to try to understand where the consensus about professional learning is. This means that, however plausible or implausible, useful or not, we find particular theories, we can consider what they contribute collectively to informing our facilitation of professional learning in ITE.

On what do theories of professional learning agree?

The importance of different forms of knowledge

Most of the theories in this book agree that professional learning cannot confine itself to considering codified knowledge or knowledge that can easily be called explicitly to mind to be reflected on rationally. A theory of professional learning has to recognise the importance of other forms of knowledge such as tacit knowledge that might be acquired without us being conscious of it. It also needs to consider the importance of factors like values and identity in the process of professional formation and to recognise that being able to produce skilled performance is the end goal of all professional learning experiences.

Several of the theories put particular emphasis on importance of integrating different forms of knowledge for the process of professional learning. Clinical practice models, PCK, Eraut's professional learning and craft models all consider the ways in which knowledge in different forms, perhaps from different sources, has to be integrated in order to be useable in professional practice. In simple apprenticeship or communities of practice models of learning, these forms of knowledge may already be integrated as they are learned. However, in approaches to learning that make use of different sources of knowledge (for example, school/university, experience/reading), it is important not to underestimate the amount of work that is needed to integrate different forms of knowledge. This cannot necessarily be left to the individual learner but needs to be built into the learning experiences that are planned for learners.

Planned and structured participation in practice

There is broad agreement that the most effective way of developing tacit and integrated forms of knowledge is through sustained participation in practice. However, it is also broadly agreed that simply putting learners in a professional practice context, for a sustained period of time, is not in itself enough. Careful consideration needs to be given to the nature of professional learning through participation in practice and experiences need to be planned to maximise their benefit. This planning includes:

» recognising the status of learners as learners rather than expecting them to participate fully too early;

» giving proper time and space for learning rather than just practising;

» structuring participation carefully on the basis of a robust developmental model of professional practice;

» sustained close collaboration with experienced practitioners;

» ensuring a helpful 'horizon of visibility' for learners in relation to the work of skilled practitioners;

» planning ways of making tacit knowledge accessible to learners;

» supporting the process of integration of different forms of knowledge;

» valuing academic learning and certification;

» recognising the importance of a wider or longer-term view than the professional competence necessary to complete the specific role that a learner has been given at this time;

» considering how the daily practice of experienced practitioners supports, or otherwise, the learning of novices.

The importance of established working culture and practices

The last bullet point, above, relates to another area of broad agreement: that the established culture of daily practice is a key determinant in how successfully novices will learn. Where daily practice is collaborative with an 'enquiring stance' that values different perspectives, novices learning will be enhanced. Where established daily practice is individualistic and/or prefers routine over enquiry and development, novices learning will be hindered. In broader terms, the patterns of interaction in a workplace and the nature of relationships between practitioners will set the context that either helps or hinders learning.

Learning as a social rather than individual process

The relationship between the organisation and nature of daily practice and the success of novices' learning draws our attention to another broad similarity between the theories in this book. For the most part they emphasise learning as a social process rather than one that we should consider as happening solely 'in the head' of learners. For this reason, if we find that learners have difficulties, rather than locating the problem in the learners we should look at the social interaction and contexts in which learning is supposed to take place to see whether changes to these might produce better outcomes.

IN A **NUTSHELL**

Recent theories of professional learning share many insights in common. These include:

» the importance of integrating diverse forms of knowledge;

» the centrality of sustained participation in practice for learning;

» awareness that putting novices in practice contexts is not in itself enough to produce adequate learning;

» learning is social not individual;

» awareness that wider established cultures of practice are an important determinant of effective professional learning.

REFLECTIONS ON **CRITICAL ISSUES**

What all the theories in this book teach us is that professional learning is a complex process. Because it is complex it is one that cannot be left to chance. To maximise the value of professional learning opportunities we need to carefully design them and actively facilitate them. This requires the involvement of people who have a good understanding of the professional learning process. We need to value such people and recognise their particular expertise as important not only for the future of individual learners but also for the practice of a whole profession.

Following on from this observation, it is important not to separate the learning of novices from the wider established culture and practices of experienced practitioners. Effective professional learning is fostered by effective established cultures of professional practice and enquiry. This means that if we want to use practice context as a resource for learners we might need to consider how we need to change the nature of practice in that context.

> *The complexity of the process and the need to connect it to effective established cultures of practice means that professional learning, if it is to be high quality, cannot be done 'on the cheap'. It needs planning, time, commitment and resources if it is to be effective.*

REFERENCES

Abell, S K (2008) Twenty Years Later: Does Pedagogical Content Knowledge Remain a Useful Idea? *International Journal of Science Education*, 30(10): 1405–16.

Aldrich, R (1999) The Apprentice in History, in Ainley, P and Rainbird, H (eds) *Apprenticeship: Towards a New Paradigm of Learning*. London: Kogan Page.

Alter, J and Coggshall, J G (2009) *Teaching as a Clinical Profession: Implications for Teacher Preparation and State Policy*. [online] Available at: http://www.gtlcenter.org/sites/default/files/docs/clinicalPractice.pdf (last accessed 21 July 2014).

Anderson, M J and Freebody, K (2005) Developing Communities of Praxis: Bridging the Theory Practice Divide in Teacher Education. *McGill Journal of Education*, 47(3): 359–78.

Argyris, C (1976) Single-Loop and Double-Loop Models in Research on Decision Making. *Administrative Science Quarterly*, 21(3): 363–75.

Argyris, C (1999) *Organisational Learning*. London: Wiley Blackwell.

Argyris, C and Schön, D A (1978) *Organizational Learning: A theory of Action Perspective*. Reading, MA: Addison-Wesley.

Arnold, J, Edwards, T, Hooley, N and Williams, J (2012) Theorising On-site Teacher Education: Philosophical Project Knowledge. *Asia-Pacific Journal of Teacher Education*, 40(1): 67–78.

Avis, J (2009) Transformation or Transformism: Engeström's Version of Activity Theory. *Educational Review*, 61(2): 151–65.

Ayvazo, S and Ward, P (2011) Pedagogical Content Knowledge of Experienced Teachers in Physical Education. *Research Quarterly for Exercise and Sport*, 82(4): 675–84.

Bakhurst, D (2009) Reflections on Activity Theory. *Educational Review*, 61(2): 197–210.

Ball, D L (2000) Bridging Practices: Intertwining Content and Pedagogy in Teaching and Learning to Teach. *Journal of Teacher Education*, 51: 241–47.

Ball, D L and Bass, H (2000) Interweaving Content and Pedagogy in Teaching and Learning to Teach: Knowing and Using Mathematics, in Boaler, J (ed) *Multiple Perspectives on the Teaching and Learning of Mathematics*. Westport: Ablex.

Barab, S A, Barnett, M and Squire, K (2002) Developing an Empirical Account of a Community of Practice: Characterising the Essential Tensions. *The Journal of the Learning Sciences*, 11(4): 489–542.

Benton, P (ed) (1990) *The Oxford Internship Scheme: Integration and Partnership in Initial Teacher Education*. London: Calouste Gulbenkian.

BERA-RSA (2014) Research and the Teaching Profession: Building Capacity for a Self-Improving Education System. [online] Available at: www.bera.ac.uk (last accessed 21 July 2014).

Biesta, G J J (2010) Why 'What Works' Still Won't Work: from Evidence-Based Education to Value-Based Education. *Studies in the Philosophy of Education*, 29: 491–503.

Billett, S (1996) Towards a Model of Workplace Learning: the Learning Curriculum. *Studies in Continuing Education*, 18(1): 43–58.

Billett, S (1998) Constructing Vocational Knowledge: Situations and Other Social Sources. *Journal of Education and Work*, 11(3): 255–73.

Billett, S (2007) Including the Missing Subject: Placing the Personal within the Community, in Hughes, J, Jewson, N, and Unwin, L (eds) *Communities of Practice: Critical Perspectives*. London: Routledge.

Black-Hawkins and Florian (2012) Classroom Teachers' Craft Knowledge of Their Inclusive Practice. *Teachers and Teaching: Theory and Practice*, 18(5): 567–84.

Bowe, R Gewirtz, S and Ball, S J (1994) Captured by the Discourse? Issues and Concerns in Researching Parental Choice, *British Journal of Sociology of Education*, 15(1): 63–78.

Broudy, H S, Smith, B D and Burnett, J (1964) *Democracy and Excellence in American Secondary Education*. Chicago: Rand McNally.

Brown, J S and Duguid, P (1991) Organizational Learning and Communities of Practice: Towards a Unified View of Working, Learning and Innovation. *Organization Science*, 2(1): 40–57.

Brown, J S and Duguid, P (2001) *The Social Life of Information*. Cambridge: Harvard Business School Press.

Brown, J S, Collins, A and Duguid, P (1989) Situated Cognition and the Culture of Learning. *Educational Researcher*, 18 (1): 32–42.

Bruner, J (1990) *Acts of Meaning*. Cambridge: Harvard University Press.

Bullough, R V (2001) Pedagogical Content Knowledge Circa 1907 and 1987: A Study in the History of an Idea. *Teaching and Teacher Education*, 17: 655–66.

Burn, K and Mutton, T (2013) *Review of 'Research-Informed Clinical Practice' in Initial Teacher Education*. [online] Available at: http://www.bera.ac.uk/wp-content/uploads/2014/02/BERA-Paper-4-Research-informed-clinical-practice.pdf (accessed 21 July 2014).

Burney, D (2004) Craft Knowledge: The Road to Transforming Schools. *Phi Delta Kappan*, 85(7): 526–31.

Carlsen, W S (1999) Domains of Teacher Knowledge, in Gess-Newsome, J. and Lederman, N.G (eds) *PCK and Science Education*. Amsterdam: Kluwer Academic Publishers.

City, E A, Elmore, R F, Fiarman, S E, and Teitel, L (2009) *Instructional Rounds in Education: A Network Approach to Improving Teaching and Learning*. Cambridge, Massachusetts: Harvard Education Press.

Clandinin, D J and Connelly, F M (1995) *Teachers' Professional Knowledge Landscapes*. New York: Teachers College Press.

Cochran, K F, DeRuiter, J A and King, R A (1993) Pedagogical Content Knowledge: An Integrated Mode for Teacher Preparation. *Journal of Teacher Education*, 44(4): 263–72.

Cochran, K F, King, R A and DeRuiter, J A, (1991) Pedagogical Content Knowledge: A Tentative Model for Teacher Preparation. Paper presented at the Annual Meeting of the American Educational Research Association, 3–7 April.

Cochran-Smith, M (1991) Learning to Teach against the Grain. *Harvard Educational Review*, 51: 279–310.

Conroy, J, Hulme, M and Menter, I (2013) Developing a 'Clinical' Model for Teacher Education. *Journal of Education for Teaching: International Research and Pedagogy*, 39(5): 557–73.

Daniel, G R, Auhl, G and Hastings, W (2013) Collaborative Feedback and Reflection for Professional Growth: Preparing First-Year Pre-Service Teachers for Participation in the Community of Practice. *Asia-Pacific Journal of Teacher Education*, 41(2): 159–72.

Daniels, H (2004) Cultural Historical Activity Theory and Professional Learning, *International Journal of Disability. Development and Education*, 51(2): 185–200.

Darling-Hammond, L (2006) *Powerful Teacher Education: Lessons from Exemplary Programmes*. San Francisco, CA: Jossey-Bass.

De Jong, O, Van Driel, J H and Verloop, N (2005) Preservice Teachers' Pedagogical Content Knowledge of using Particle Models in Teaching Chemistry. *Journal of Research in Science Teaching*, 42(8): 947–64.

Douglas, A S (2014) *Student Teachers in School Practice: An Analysis of Learning Opportunities*. London: Palgrave MacMillan.

Douglas, A S and Ellis, V (2011) Connecting Does Not Necessarily Mean Learning: Course Handbooks as Mediating Tools in School-University Partnerships. *Journal of Teacher Education*, 62(5): 465–76.

Drechsler, M and Van Driel, J (2008) Experienced Teachers' Pedagogical Content Knowledge of Teaching Acid-Based Chemistry. *Research in Science Education*, 38: 611–31.

Dreyfus, H L and Dreyfus S E (1986) *Mind over Machine: The Power of Human Intuition and Expertise in the Era of the Computer*. Oxford: Basil Blackwell.

Edwards, A and Daniels, H (2004) Editorial. *Educational Review*, 56(2): 107–11.

Ellis, V, Edwards, A and Smagorinsky, P (eds) (2010) *Cultural-Historical Perspectives on Teacher Education and Development: Learning Teaching*. London: Routledge.

Engeström, Y (1987) *Learning by Expanding: An Activity-Theoretical Approach to Developmental Research*. Helsinki: Orienta-Konsultit.

Engeström, Y (1990). When is a tool? Multiple meanings of artifacts in human activity, in Engeström, Y, *Learning, Working and Imagining: Twelve Studies in Activity Theory*. Helsinki: Orienta-Konsultit.

Engeström, Y (1996) Developmental Studies of Work as a Testbench of Activity Theory, in Chaiklin, S and Lave, J (eds) *Understanding Practice: Perspectives on Activity and Context*. Cambridge: Cambridge University Press.

Engeström, Y (2001) Making Expansive Decisions: An Activity-Theoretical Study of Practiotioners Building Collaborative Medical Care for Children, in Allwood, C M and Selart, M (eds) *Decision Making: Social and Creative Dimensions*. Dordrecht: Kluwer Academic.

Engeström, Y (2007) From Communities of Practice to Mycorrhizae, in Hughes, J, Jewson, N, and Unwin, L (eds) *Communities of Practice: Critical Perspectives*. London: Routledge.

Engeström, Y and Glaveanu, V (2012), On Third Generation Activity Theory: Interview with Yrjö Engeström. *Europe's Journal of Psychology*, 8(4): 515–18.

Engeström, Y and Miettinen, R (1999) Introduction, in Engeström, Y, Miettinen, R and Punamaki, R-L (eds) *Perspectives on Activity Theory*. Cambridge: Cambridge University Press.

Engeström, Y, Miettinen, R and Punamaki, R-L (eds) (1999) *Perspectives on Activity Theory*. Cambridge: Cambridge University Press.

Engeström, Y, Virkunnen, J, Helle, M, Pihlaja, J and Poikela, R (1996) Change Laboratory as a Tool for Transforming Work. *Lifelong Learning in Europe*, 1(2): 10–17.

Eraut, M (1985) Knowledge Creation and Knowledge Use in Professional Context. *Studies in Higher Education*, 10(2): 117–33.

Eraut, M (1994) *Developing Professional Knowledge and Competence*. London: Routledge.

Eraut. M (2000a) Teacher Education Designed or Framed, *International Journal of Educational Research*, 33: 557–74.

Eraut, M (2000b) Non-Formal Learning and Tacit Knowledge in Professional Work. *British Journal of Educational Psychology*, 70: 113–36.

Eraut, M (2002) Conceptual Analysis and Research Questions: Do the Concepts of 'Learning Community' and 'Community of Practice' Provide Added Value? Paper presented at the Annual Meeting of the American Educational Research Association, 1–5 April.

Eraut, M (2004a) Informal Learning in the Workplace. *Studies in Continuing Education*, 26(2): 247–72.

Eraut, M (2004b) Transfer of Knowledge between Education and Workplace Settings, in Rainbird, H, Fuller, A and Munro, A (eds) *Workplace Learning in Context*. London: Routledge.

Eraut, M (2007) Learning from Other People in the Workplace. *Oxford Review of Education*, 33(4): 403–22.

Eraut, M (2010) Knowledge, Working Practices, and Learning, in Billett, S (ed) *Learning through Practice*, Professional and Practice-based Learning 1, Springer Science and Business Media.

Eraut, M (2012) Developing a Broader Approach to Professional Learning, in McKee, A and Eraut, M (eds) *Learning Trajectories, Innovation and Identity for Professional Development*, Innovation and Change in Professional Education 7. Springer Science and Business Media.

Eraut, M (2014) Developing Knowledge for Qualified Professionals, in McNamara, O, Murray, J and Jones, M (eds) *Workplace Learning in Teacher Education: International Policy and Practice*. London: Springer.

Eraut, M and Hirsh, W (2007) *The Significance of Workplace Learning for Individual's, Groups and Organisations*, SKOPE Monograph 9, Pembroke College, Oxford.

Evans, K, Hodkinson, P, Rainbird, H and Unwin L (2006) *Improving Workplace Learning*. London: Routledge.

Fernandez-Balboa, J-M and Stiehl, J (1995) The Generic Nature of Pedagogical Content Knowledge among College Professors. *Teaching and Teacher Education*, 11(3): 293–306.

Festinger, L (1957) *A Theory of Cognitive Dissonance*. Stanford: Stanford University Press.

Foucault, M (2001) *The Order of Things: Archaeology of the Human Sciences*. London: Routledge.

Fuller, A (2007) Critiquing Theories of Learning and Communities of Practice, in Hughes, J, Jewson, N and Unwin, L (eds) *Communities of Practice: Critical Perspectives*. London: Routledge.

Fuller, A and Unwin, L (2003) Learning as Apprentices in the Contemporary UK Workplace: Creating and Managing Expansive and Restrictive Participation. *Journal of Education and Work*, 16(4): 407–26.

Fuller, A, Hodkinson, H, Hodkinson, P and Unwin, L (2005) Learning as Peripheral Participation in Communities of Practice: A Reassessment of Key Concepts in Workplace Learning. *British Educational Research Journal*, 31(1): 49–68.

Furlong, J and Maynard, T (1995) *Mentoring Student Teachers: The Growth of Professional Knowledge*. London: Routledge.

Gamble, J (2001) Modelling the Invisible: the Pedagogy of Craft Apprenticeship. *Studies in Continuing Education*, 23(2): 185–200.

Gess-Newsome, J (1999) Pedagogical Content Knowledge: An Introduction and Orientation, in J Gess-Newsome and N G Lederman (eds) *Examining Pedagogical Content Knowledge*. Dordrecht: Kluwer Academic Publishers.

Gherardi, S and Nicolini, D and Odella, F (1998) Toward a Social Understanding of How People Learn in Organizations: the Notion of Situated Curriculum. *Management Learning*, 29: 273–97.

Grimmett, P P, Fleming, R and Trotter, L (2009) Legitimacy and Identity in Teacher Education: A Micro-Political Struggle Constrained by Macro-Political Pressures. *Asia-Pacific Journal of Teacher Education*, 37(1): 5–26.

Grimmett, P P and MacKinnon, A M (1992) Craft Knowledge and the Education of Teachers. *Review of Research in Education*, 18: 385–456.

Grossman, P L (1989) A Study in Contrast: Sources of Pedagogical Content Knowledge for Secondary English. *Journal of Teacher Education*, 40: 24–31.

Grossman, P L (1991) Overcoming the Apprenticeship of Observation in Teacher Education Coursework. *Teaching and Teacher Education*, 7(4): 345–57.

Grossman, P (2010) Learning to Practice: The Design of Clinical Experience in Teacher Preparation. [online] Available at: http://www.nea.org/assets/docs/Clinical_Experience_-_Pam_Grossman.pdf (accessed 21 July 2014).

Grossman, P, Hammerness, K and McDonald, M (2009) Redefining Teaching, Re-imagining Teacher Education. *Teachers and Teaching: Theory and Practice*, 15(2): 273–89.

Gudmundsdottir, S (1990) Values in Pedagogical Content Knowledge, *Journal of Teacher Education*, 41(2): 44–52.

Gudmundsdottir, S (1991) Ways of Seeing Are Ways of Knowing. The Pedagogical Content Knowledge of an Expert English Teacher. *Journal of Curriculum Studies*, 23(5): 409–21.

Gudmundsdottir, S and Shulman, L S (1987) Pedagogical Content Knowledge in Social Studies. *Scandinavian Journal of Educational Research*, 31(2): 59–70.

Hagger, H and McIntyre, D (2006) *Learning Teaching from Teachers: Realizing the Potential of School-Based Teacher Education*. Maidenhead: Open University Press.

Hammersley, M (2005) The Myth of Research-based Practice: The Critical case of Educational Inquiry. *International Journal of Social Research Methodology*, 8(4): 317–30.

Haston, W and Leon-Guerrero, A (2008) Sources of Pedagogical Content Knowledge: Reports by Preservice Instrumental Music Teachers. *Journal of Music Teacher Education*, 17(2): 48–59.

Hazard, R H, Chandler, B J and Stiles, L J (1967) The Tutorial and Clinical Program for Teacher Education. *Journal of Teacher Education*, 18(3): 269–76.

Henze, I, Van Driel, J H and Verloop, N (2008) Development of Experienced Science Tecahers' Pedagogical Content Knowledge of Models of the Solar System and the Universe. *International Journal of Science Education*, 30(10): 1321–42.

Hodges, D C (1998) Participation as Dis-identification with/in a Community of Practice. *Mind, Culture and Activity*, 5(4): 272–90.

Hodkinson, H and Hodkinson, P (2004a) Rethinking the Concept of Community of Practice in Relation to Schoolteachers' Workplace Learning. *International Journal of Training and Development*, 8(1): 21–31.

Hodkinson, P and Hodkinson, H (2004b) The Significance of Individuals' Dispositions in Workplace Learning: A Case Study of Two Teachers. *Journal of Education and Work*, 17(2): 167–82.

Honey, P and Mumford, A, (1982) *Manual of Learning Styles*. Maidenhead: Peter Honey Publishing.

Hughes, J (2007) Lost in Translation: Communities of Practice; The Journey from Academic Model to Practitioner Tool, in Hughes, J, Jewson, N and Unwin, L (eds) *Communities of Practice: Critical Perspectives*. London: Routledge.

Hughes, J, Jewson, N and Unwin, L (2007) *Communities of Practice: Critical Perspectives*. London: Routledge.

Hutchins, E. (1996) Learning To Navigate, in Chaiklin, S and Lave, J (eds) *Understanding Practice*. Cambridge: Cambridge University Press.

Jahreie, C. F. (2010). Making Sense of Cultural Tools in Case Work: Student Teachers' Participation Trajectory. *Teaching and Teacher Education*, 26(6): 1229–37.

Jewson, N. (2007) Cultivating Network Analysis: Rethinking the Concept of 'Community', in Hughes, J. Jewson, N. and Unwin, L. (2007) *Communities of Practice: Critical Perspectives*. London: Routledge.

Keller, C and Keller, J D (1996) Thinking and Acting with Iron, in Chaiklin, S. and Lave, J. (eds) *Understanding Practice*. Cambridge: Cambridge University Press.

Kelly, A (2006) 'Too Busy to Think, Too Tired to Learn': The Attrition of the Apprenticeship Model of Surgical Training in the United Kingdom. *Educate: The Journal of Doctoral Learning in Education*, 1(1): 45–65.

Kind, V (2009) Potential Content Knowledge in Science Education: Perspectives and Potential for Progress. *Studies in Science Education*, 45(2): 169–204.

Kolb, D A (1983) *Experiential Learning: Experience as the Source of Learning and Development*. London: Prentice Hall.

Kolokouri, E, Theodoraki, X, and Plakitsi, K (2013) A Cultural Historical Activity Theory Approach in Natural Sciences Education Laboratory Lessons. *World Journal of Education*, 2(2): 23–40.

Kriewaldt, J and Turnidge, D (2013) Conceptualising an Approach to Clinical Reasoning in the Education Profession. *Australian Journal of Teacher Education*, 38(6): 103–15.

Kuhn, T S (1996) *The Structure of Scientific Revolutions*. Chicago: University of Chicago Press.

Lave, J (1996) Teaching as Learning, in Practice. *Mind Culture and Society*, 3(3): 149–64.

Lave, J and Wenger, E (1991) *Situated Learning: Legitimate Peripheral Participation*. Cambridge: Cambridge University Press.

Lederman, N G and Gess-Newsome, J (1992) Do Subject Matter Knowledge, Pedagogical Knowledge and Pedagogical Content Knowledge Constitute the Idea Gas Law of Science Teaching? *Journal of Science Teacher Education*, 3(1): 16–20.

Leinhardt, G (1990) Capturing Craft Knowledge in Teaching. *Educational Researcher*, 19(2): 18–25.

Li, L C, Grimshaw, J M, Nielsen, C, Judd, M, Coyte, P C and Graham, I D (2009) Evolution of Wenger's Concept of Community of Practice. [online] Available at: http://www.implementationscience.com/content/4/1/11 (accessed 10 October 2014).

Liu, S (2013) Pedagogical Content Knowledge: A Case Study of ESL Teacher Educator. *English Language Teaching*, 6(7): 128–38.

Loughran, J, Berry, A and Mulhall, P (2006) *Understanding and Developing Science Teachers' Pedagogical Content Knowledge*. Rotterdam: Sense Publishers.

Loughran, J, Mulhall, P and Berry, A (2008) Exploring Pedagogical Content Knowledge in Science Teacher Education. *International Journal of Science Education*, 30(10): 1301–20.

Marshall, H (1972) Structural Constraints on Learning, in Greer, B (ed) *Learning to Work*. Beverley Hills, CA: Sage.

Martin, D and Peim, N (2009) Critical Perspectives on Activity Theory. *Educational Review*, 61(2): 131–38.

Marx, K (1894/1992) *Capital: Critique of Political Economy, Volume 3*. London: Penguin.

Mason, C L (1999) The TRIAD Approach: A Consensus for Science Teaching and Learning, in J Gess-Newsome and N G Lederman (eds) *Examining Pedagogical Content Knowledge*. Dordrecht: Kluwer Academic Publishers.

Maynard, T (2001) The Student Teacher and the Community of Practice: A Consideration of Learning as Participation. *Cambridge Journal of Education*, 31(1): 39–52.

McIntosh, E G (1971) The Clinical Approach to Teacher Education. *Journal of Teacher Education*, 22(1): 18–24.

McLean Davies, L, Anderson, M, Deans, J, Dinham, S, Griffin, P, Kameniar, B, Page, J, Reid, C, Rickards, F, Taylor, C and Tyler, D (2013) Masterly Preparation: Embedding Clinical Practice in a Graduate Pre-Service Teacher Education Programme. *Journal of Education for Teaching: International Research and Pedagogy*. 39(1): 93–106.

McNamara, D and Desforges, C (1978) The Social Sciences, Teacher Education and the Objectification of Craft Knowledge. *British Journal of Teacher Education: International Research and Pedagogy*, 4(1): 17–36.

McNamara, D and Desforges, C (1979) Theory and Practice: Methodological Procedures for the Objectification of Craft Knowledge. *British Journal of Teacher Education: International Research and Pedagogy*, 5(2): 145–52.

McNamara O, Murray, J and Jones, M (eds) (2014) *Workplace Learning in Teacher Education; International Policy and Practice*. London: Springer.

McNicholl, J and Blake, A (2013) Transforming Teacher Education, an Activity Theory Analysis. *Journal of Education for Teaching: International Research and Pedagogy*, 39(3): 281–300.

McNicholl, J, Childs, A and Burn, K (2013) School Subject Departments as Sites for Science Teachers' Learning Pedagogical Content Knowledge. *Teacher Development: An International Journal Of Teachers' Professional Development*, 17(2): 155–75.

Millican, J S (2013) Describing Instrumental Music Teachers' Thinking: Implications for Understanding Pedagogical Content Knowledge. *Update: Applications of Research in Music Education*, 31: 45–53.

Monte-Sano, C (2011) Learning to Open Up History for Students. *Journal of Teacher Education*, 62(3): 260–72.

NCATE (2010) *Transforming Teacher Education through Clinical Practice: A National Strategy To Prepare Effective Teachers*. [online] Available at: http://www.ncate.org/LinkClick.aspx?fileticket=zzeiB1OoqPk%3D&t abid=715 (accessed 21 July 2014).

OECD (2011) *Building a High Quality Teaching Profession: Lessons from around the World*. [online] Available at: http://www.oecd.org/edu/school/programmeforinternationalstudentassessmentpisa/buildingahigh-qualityt eachingprofessionlessonsfromaroundtheworld.htm (accessed 23 July 2014).

Ormrod, J E and Cole, D B (1996) Teaching Content Knowledge and Pedagogical Content Knowledge: A Model from Geographic Education. *Journal of Teacher Education*, 47(1): 37–42.

Orr, J E (1996) *Talking about Machines: An Ethnography of a Modern Job*. Ithaca, NY: ILR Press.

Palincsar, A (1999) Response: A Community of Practice. *Teacher Education and Special Education: The Journal of the Teacher education Division of the Council for Exceptional Children*, 22: 272–74.

Palincsar, A S, Magnusson, S J, Marano, N, Ford, D and Brown, N (1998) Designing a Community of Practice: Principles and Practices of the GIsML Community. *Teaching and Teacher Education*, 14(1): 5–19.

Phelps, G and Schilling, S (2004) Developing Measures of Content Knowledge for Teaching Reading. *The Elementary School Journal*, 105(1): 31–48.

Philpott, C (2006) Transfer of Learning between Higher Education Institution and School Based Components of PGCE Courses. *Journal of Vocational Education and Training*, 58(3): 283–302.

Potari, D (2013) The Relationship of Theory and Practice in Mathematics Teacher Professional Development: An Activity Theory Perspective. *ZDM Mathematics Education*, 45: 507–19.

Reason, P and Bradbury, H (2001) *Handbook of Action Research: Participative Inquiry and Practice*. London: Sage.

Rigano, D and Ritchie, S (1999) Learning the Craft: A Student Teacher's Story. *Asia-Pacific Journal of Teacher Education*, 27(2): 127–42.

Rikowski, G (1999) Nietzsche, Marx and Mastery: The Learning unto Death, in Ainley, P and Rainbird, H (eds) *Apprenticeship: Towards a New Paradigm of Learning*. London: Kogan Page.

Roegman, R and Riehl, C (2012) Playing Doctor With Education: Considerations in Using Medical Rounds as a Model for Instructional Rounds. *Journal of School Leadership*, 22: 922–52.

Rogoff, B (1990) *Apprenticeship in Thinking: Cognitive Development in Social Context*. Oxford: Oxford University Press.

Roth, W-M (2004) Introduction: Activity Theory and Education: An Introduction. *Mind, Culture and Activity*, 11(1): 1–8.

Roth, W-M and Lee, Y-J (2007) 'Vygotsky's Neglected Legacy': Cultural-Historical Activity Theory. *Review of Educational Research*, 77(2): 186–232.

Roth, W-M and Tobin, K (2002) Redesigning an 'Urban' Teacher Education Programme: An Activity Theory Perspective. *Mind, Culture and Activity*, 9(2): 108–31.

Sanchez, H S and Borg, S (2014) Insights into L2 Teachers' Pedagogical Content Knowledge: A Cognitive Perspective on Their Grammar Explanations. *System*, 44: 45–53.

Schön, D A (1990) *Educating the Reflective Practitioner: Toward a New Design for Teaching and Learning in the Professions*. London: Wiley.

Schön, D A (1993) Generative Metaphor, in Ortony, A (ed) *Metaphor and Thought*. Cambridge. Cambridge University Press.

Schön, D A (1994) *The Reflective Practitioner: How Professionals Think in Action*. Farnham: Ashgate.

Schwab, J T (1958) On the Corruption of Education by Psychology. *The School Review*, 66(2): 169–84.

Schwab, J T (1969) The Practical: A Language for Curriculum. *The School Review*, 78(1): 1–23.

Schwab, J T (1971) The Practical: Arts Of Eclectic. *The School Review*, 79(4): 493–542.

Schwab, J T (1973) The Practical 3: Translation into Curriculum. *The School Review*, 81(4): 501–22.

Sennett, R (2008) *The Craftsman*. London: Allen Lane.

Shimahara, N K (1998) The Japanese Model of Professional Development: Teaching as Craft. *Teaching and Teacher Education*, 14(5): 451–62.

Shulman, L S (1986) Those Who Understand: Knowledge Growth in Teaching. *Educational Researcher*, 15(4): 4–14.

Shulman, L S (1987) Knowledge and Teaching: Foundations of the New Reform. *Harvard Educational Review*, 57(1): 1–22.

Shulman, L S (2005) The Signature Pedagogies of the Professions of Law, Medicine, Engineering, and the Clergy: Potential Lessons for the Education of Teachers. Delivered at the Math Science Partnerships (MSP) Workshop: 'Teacher Education for Effective Teaching and Learning', hosted by the National Research Council's Center for Education, February 6–8, 2005, Irvine, California.

Sim, C (2006) Preparing for Professional Experiences: Incorporating Pre-Service Teachers as 'Communities of Practice'. *Teaching and Teacher Education*, 22: 77–83.

Snoek, M (2013) From Splendid Isolation to Crossed Boundaries? The Futures Of Teacher Education in the Light of Activity Theory. *Teacher Development: An International Journal of Teachers' Professional Development*, 17(3): 307–21.

Stamps, D (1997) Learning is Social. Training is Irrelevant? *Training*, 34(2): 34–42.

Tom, A R (1980) Teaching as a Moral Craft: A Metaphor For Teaching and Teacher Education. *Curriculum Inquiry*, 10(3): 317–23.

Trowler, P R (2005) A Sociology of Teaching, Learning and Enhancement: Improving Practices in Higher Education. *Revista de Sociologia*, 76: 13–32.

Ure, J (2010) Reforming Teacher Education through a Professionally Applied Study of Teaching. *Journal of Education for Teaching: International Research and Pedagogy*, 36(4): 461–75.

Van Driel, J H and Berry, A (2010) Pedagogical Content Knowledge, in Peterson, P, Baker, E and McGaw, B (eds) *International Encyclopaedia of Education* (3rd edition). Amsterdam: Elsevier.

Van Driel, J H and De Jong, O (2001) Investigating the Development of Preservice Teachers Pedagogical Content Knowledge. Paper presented at the Annual Meeting of the National Association for Research and Science Teaching, 3–7 April.

Van Driel, J H and Berry, A (2012) Teacher Professional Development Focusing on Pedagogical Content Knowledge. *Educational Researcher*, 41(1): 26–8.

Van Driel, J H, Veal, W R and Janssen, F J J M (2001) Pedagogical Content Knowledge: An Integrative Component within the Knowledge Base for Teaching. *Teaching and Teacher Education*, 17: 979–86.

Van Driel, J H, Verloop, N and de Vos, W (1998) Developing Science Teachers' Pedagogical Content Knowledge. *Journal of Research in Science Education*, 35(6): 673–95.

Warner, A R, Houston, RW and Cooper, J M (1977) Rethinking the Clinical Concept in Teacher Education. *Journal of Teacher Education*, 28(1): 15–18.

Wenger, E (1998) *Communities of Practice: Learning, Meaning and Identity*. Cambridge: Cambridge University Press.

Wenger, E and Snyder, W (2000) Communities of Practice: The Organizational Frontier. *Harvard* Business Review, January–February: 139–45.

Wenger, E, McDermott, R A and Snyder, W (2002) *Cultivating Communities of Practice: A Guide to Managing Knowledge.* Cambridge, MA: Harvard University Press.

Wilson, S M, Floden, R E and Ferrini-Mundy, J (2002) Teacher Preparation Research: An Insiders View from Outside. *Journal of Teacher Education*, 61(1–2): 89–99.

Wood, N (2004) Unknown Unknowns: Knowledge Elicitations for Multimedia on Craft Learning. Paper presented at Challenging Craft International Conference, Gray's School of Art, Aberdeen, Scotland, 8–10 September.

Wood, N (2006) *Transmitting Craft Knowledge: Designing Interactive Media to Support Tacit Skills Learning,* PhD thesis, Sheffield Hallam University. [online] Available at: http://shura.shu.ac.uk/3202/ (accessed 18 August 2014).

Zeichner, K (2010) Rethinking the Connections between Campus Courses and Field Experiences in College- And University-Based Teacher Education. *Journal of Teacher Education*, 53(3): 190–204.

Zembylas, M (2007) Emotional Ecology: The Intersection Of Emotional Knowledge and Pedagogical Content Knowledge in Teaching. *Teaching and Teacher Education*, 23: 355–67.

Zuboff, S (1988) *In the Age of the Smart Machine: The Future of Work and Power.* Oxford: Heinemann.

INDEX

A

ambivalence, 65
application deficit, 62
application, mode of knowledge, 29
apprenticeship
    cognitive, 66
    criticism, 69
    definition, 65
    Initial Teacher Education, 69–71
    teacher education, 68–69
Argyris learning model
    demand side learning, 12
    double-loop learning, 8–9
    reflection on conceptualisation, 10–11
    reflection-in-action, 12
    single-loop learning, 8
    supply side learning, 12
    theory and practice relationships, 11–12
association, mode of knowledge, 29
authoritative knowledge, 9, 10

B

boundary crossing, 43
business context, community of practice, 38

C

canonical communities of practice, 39
CHAT *see* Cultural Historical Activity Theory
clinical practice models
    assessment on pupils, 57
    client focus, 56
    clinical reasoning, 57
    communities of enquiry, 58–59
    conceptual challenges, 61–62
    feedback frequency and quality, 59
    fragmentation, 59
    Initial Teacher Education, 55
    inter-institutional and intra-institutional
       changes, 60
    ITE to CPD continuum, 59
    nature of schools, 59
    organisational and cultural changes, 60
    practical challenges, 60–61
    quality of school experience, 57–58
    regulatory and legal problems, 61
    research evidence, 61
    resource issues, 61
    robust evidence base, 60
    roles in ITE, 58
    scalable and sustainable, 61
    school experience, 56
clinical reasoning

    authentic development of, 57
    definiton of, 56
    robust evidence base, 60
codified knowledge, 27, 67
cognitive apprenticeship, 66
collaborative working, 32
communities of practice
    boundary crossing, 43
    business context, 38
    canonical, 39
    challenges to ITE, 40–41
    coherence of, 37–38
    descriptive, 37
    empirically driven, 37
    expansive learning, 43
    formulations of, 37
    foster learning, 38–40
    implications for ITE, 41–44
    intergenerational encounters, 39
    legitimate peripheral participation, 37, 42
    membership, 39
    non-canonical, 39
    normativity, 38
    power and conflict, 39
    practice as community, 36
    restrictive learning, 43
    social constructivism, 39
    students as teachers, 42
    theoretically driven, 37
craft
    as professional, 64
    definition, 64
    teaching as, 67–68
craftsmanship, 64, 65
Cultural Historical Activity Theory (CHAT), 37
    activity, actions and operations, 47–48
    coherence of, 50–52
    definition, 2
    empirical evidence, 50
    first generation, 45–47
    ideology, 51
    individual learner differences, 52
    second generation, 47–48
    subject, object and tool relationships, 45–47
    teacher education, 52–53
    third generation, 48–50
    Western education, 45
cultural knowledge, 26
curricular knowledge, 15

D

demand side learning, 12
descriptive community of practice, 37
double-loop learning

86